Dealing with Diversity

RELIGION AND DEMOCRACY
Reconceptualizing Religion, Culture, and Politics in a Global Context

Series Editor

Aakash Singh Rathore is a Visiting Professor at the School of Social Sciences, Jawaharlal Nehru University, New Delhi, an International Fellow at the Center for Ethics and Global Politics, Luiss University, Rome, and Director of the International Research Network on Religion and Democracy (IRNRD), New York City.

This series is dedicated to the memory of Peter Losonczi (1970–2015), the series' original editor and founder of IRNRD.

Other Books in the Series

Military Chaplaincy in an Era of Religious Pluralism: Military–Religious Nexus in Asia, Europe, and USA
Torkel Brekke and Vladimir Tikhonov (Eds)

Europe, India, and the Limits of Secularism
Jakob De Roover

Secularism, Religion, and Democracy in Southeast Asia
Vidhu Verma (Ed.)

Dealing with Diversity

A Study in Contemporary Liberalism

DOMENICO MELIDORO

OXFORD
UNIVERSITY PRESS

OXFORD
UNIVERSITY PRESS

Oxford University Press is a department of the University of Oxford.
It furthers the University's objective of excellence in research, scholarship,
and education by publishing worldwide. Oxford is a registered trademark of
Oxford University Press in the UK and in certain other countries.

Published in India by
Oxford University Press
22 Workspace, 2nd Floor, 1/22 Asaf Ali Road, New Delhi 110 002, India

ISBN-13 (print edition): 978-0-19-012113-6
ISBN-10 (print edition): 0-19-012113-0

ISBN-13 (eBook): 978-0-19-099126-5
ISBN-10 (eBook): 0-19-099126-7

Typeset in ScalaPro 9.5/13
by The Graphics Solution, New Delhi 110 092
Printed in India by Replika Press Pvt. Ltd

To Claudio,
to his rare and precious words

Contents

Series Note

During the last two decades, the formerly dominant status of the secularist paradigm has been undermined globally. Recent developments across different regions of the world (the Indian subcontinent, the Arab world, Europe) bear far-reaching political consequences, both within the regional as well as the global scenarios. Some authors, formerly secularists, speak of the emergence of a postsecular era, and it is by now a generally shared realization that the influence of religion can no longer be ignored as a determinative factor in the contemporary socio-cultural and political constellation. Reflecting on these developments, both in social and political science, an intensive body of work has been developing that addresses the complicated and dynamic nexus between components of these processes—religion(s), secularization, democratization, modernization, cultural transformations—in order to better understand and interpret the rapidly changing realities. Moreover, the process(es) of globalization and the consequences of the postcolonial condition make the exchanges and the mutual influences amongst world regions unprecedentedly rapid and intense. As a unique innovation, the series Religion and Democracy: Reconceptualizing Religion, Culture, and Politics in a Global Context combines interdisciplinary methods with an inter-contextual focus, with a new sensitivity for the palpable relevance of religion. It includes original works of pioneering scholarship that express and reflect the thematic and theoretical variability of the fluid and dynamic situation resulting from this dual process of 'postsecularization' on the one hand and 'globalization'/'postcolonialism' on the other. The main geographical focus of the series will be South Asia, predominantly India, with an eye on the earlier-mentioned global interplay.

Aakash Singh Rathore

...Nothing's more terrible
than [diversity]. Exposed every moment
—shouted ceaselessly—incessant

exception—madness unrestrained
like a fire—contradiction
by which all justice is desecrated.

Oh, blacks, Jews, poor hosts
of the marked and different, born from
innocent wombs into sterile

springtimes, of worms and serpents,
horrendous without their knowing, condemned
to be atrociously meek, childishly violent,

hate! tear apart the world of well-born men!
Only a bloodbath can save the world
from its bourgeois dreams, certain

to make it more and more unreal!
Only a revolution that slaughters
these dead men can deconsecrate their evil!

This is what a prophet would shout who doesn't have
the strength to kill a fly—whose strength
lies in his degrading [diversity].

Only when this has been said, or shouted,
will my fate be able to free itself,
and begin my discourse on reality.[1]

---

[1] Pasolini (1996: 135–7).

Liberalism and Diversity

The Subject Matter

This book deals with the problem of diversity within liberalism. In this context, the book first looks at how existing theories have dealt with the problem of diversity, and then conceptualizes a normative framework through which liberal theory should face diversity. Thus, the book first presents the existing state of the art on liberalism and diversity, and then provides an account of the most adequate liberal solution to the issues raised by the accommodation of diversity.

With this introductory chapter, I aim to pave the way for the upcoming discussion, and, in order to accomplish this task, I will give some (unavoidably broad) definitions of the crucial notions employed hereafter, namely, liberalism and diversity.

Liberalism is a complex and differentiated tradition of political thought. Finding a definition of liberalism that might achieve a certain degree of acceptance in the international community of scholars is not an easy task. Recent attempts at finding a widely shared definition of liberalism have faced countless troubles. For instance, as Alan Ryan has remarked: whereas it is 'easy to list famous liberals, it is harder to say what they have in common'.[1] In fact, while it is beyond any doubt that John Locke, Adam Smith, John Stuart Mill, and Montesquieu deserve a place of honour in the list of venerable liberal classics, it is difficult to find something upon which they agree. The same consideration holds for

---

[1] Ryan (2012: 21).

Isaiah Berlin, John Rawls, and Ronald Dworkin as the most influential contemporary liberal theorists. The picture gets even more complicated when one tries to identify elements of continuity within the history of liberal thought. For instance, although there is some family resemblance between what Berlin and Rawls say about the welfare state or the scope of individual liberties, the likeness diminishes when we consider theorists of different historical ages, such as Montesquieu and Dworkin.[2]

In order to introduce the theoretical task I am going to undertake, and considering that any theoretical work has to start from some unjustified postulations, I will make some assumptions on what I mean by liberalism in the following pages. First, liberalism is a theory about the limits of political power. For liberals, individual freedom is a default position, and the burden of proof always lies on those who want to curb freedom. To this, I would add that the aim of liberalism is to achieve conditions of social peace and maintain it. At the risk of oversimplification, one could say that liberalism, since its inception, can be read as an attempt to give an answer to the question, 'how to live together',[3] despite the fact that people are different with regard to their ethical beliefs, religion, interests, identities, belonging, and so on.

Liberalism, thus, is the search for conditions of social peace in the face of this plurality. In addition, although it might seem obvious, I think it is worthy to remark that I assume liberalism to be a political theory.[4] Liberals distinguish the public from the private, and consider the former as the primary domain in which liberal precepts hold. The fact that liberalism is a theory that is mainly concerned with the political domain entails that it is in no way committed to the unrestricted inculcation of liberal norms in all the domains of social and individual life. Individual rights, freedoms of association, public–private distinction, and toleration are the resources at the disposal of liberalism to counteract any immediate imposition of general liberal norms within individual and collective

---

[2] See Bell (2014) for an account of the difficulties of finding a workable definition of liberalism.

[3] Audard (2009: 727).

[4] Judith Shklar (1989: 21), one of the prominent theorists to argue on the political character of liberalism, argues that liberalism is 'a political doctrine, not a philosophy of life such as has been traditionally been provided by various forms of revealed religion and other comprehensive Weltanschauungen.'

life. Even Brian Barry, whose *Culture and Equality* is generally considered as one of the most powerful advocates of the universality of the liberal values, admits that (at least in principle) it is not 'part of liberalism ... to insist that every group must conform to liberal principles in its internal structure'.[5] Nor are individuals, I would add, forced to live their lives according to the precepts of liberal theory. However, although some sort of division between the public and the private is a constitutive feature of any liberal theory, this does not exclude reciprocal influences between the two spheres of human life.[6]

Given this broad understanding of liberalism, I assume that individualism and egalitarianism are the core principles of this political theory. Liberalism is individualist in a very restricted sense, namely, in the sense that persons *uti singuli* are the basic units of moral and political consideration and that individual claims have priority over collective claims.[7] This entails, for instance, that individual liberties cannot be curtailed in order to achieve collective ends. For liberals, as John Rawls famously stated, 'liberty can be restricted only for the sake of liberty itself.'[8] A liberal theory is also egalitarian in the sense that the same moral status should be accorded to all human beings. This point requires further clarifications. Liberal egalitarianism does not concern the outcomes of a distribution of goods, resources, or opportunities. It should rather be understood as giving everyone an equal opportunity to reach her/his own aims and to realize her/his life plans in accordance with a similar freedom to all. Furthermore, liberal egalitarianism does not even amount to the view

---

[5] Barry (2001: 147).

[6] For the pervasiveness of public values and the ways in which political principles can shape also extra-political life, see Galston (1991: Chapter 13) and Macedo (1990: Chapter 2).

[7] Note that this minimal concept of individualism is different from the concept of individuality advocated by John Stuart Mill and some contemporary Millian perfectionists. Mill's individuality is concerned with the development of the self and the cultivation of human character. Further, individuality is in contrast with uncontested habits, customs, and established traditions (Mill 2003: 133). The individualism I am talking about here concerns the fact that only individuals matter, but does not take a position on which conceptions of the good are worthy to be pursued.

[8] Rawls (1999a: 214).

that all the individuals are the same, but to the more modest idea that everyone has the same dignity and that arbitrary discrimination should not be allowed.

After the definition of liberalism, I proceed by explaining what is meant by diversity in this book. Here, diversity is conceived as a *fact* that marks contemporary societies.[9] The multiplicity of beliefs, interests, identities, doctrines, loyalties, and cultural practices are simply out there, independent of our will, attitude, and conduct.[10] Stressing that diversity is considered as a mere fact means, among the other things, that it is not primarily seen as a state of affairs that should be somehow promoted or encouraged[11] for the fact it makes a society fair, progressive, and inclusive. Rather, for the purposes of this book, diversity is first and foremost a condition to be faced by liberalism. In other terms, although other ways of conceiving of diversity are not ruled out, this is a work on how liberalism faces the *fact* of diversity. It is an enquiry on some possible liberal ways of confronting diversity.[12]

As the political theorist Stephen Macedo argues, 'diversity is the great issue of our time: nationalism and religious sectarianism; a heightened consciousness of gender, race, and ethnicity; a greater assertiveness with respect to sexual orientation; and a reassertion of the religious voice in the public square.'[13] Thus, as a matter of fact, our social world is crowded

---

[9] Here, I would like to remark on the connection between diversity and some form of democracy. In general, dictatorships, authoritarian regimes, and ancient monarchies require, and thrive on, the cultural homogeneity of their peoples. On the contrary, diversity, as understood in this book, flourishes when democratic freedoms are recognized. See Tripathy and Padmanabhan (2013: 2).

[10] See Bellamy (2000), Parekh (2008: 80), and Spinner-Halev (1995).

[11] For a contrasting view, according to which diversity is a fact that 'we should celebrate, protect, and encourage', see Ten (1993: 7).

[12] This is a deliberately broad understanding of diversity. In this sense, diversity includes both *plurality* ('where things are so many variations on a theme, can be ordered and compared') and *difference* ('which supposes at least the possibility that things are incommensurable, that they cannot be part of the same space, the same table or chart'). See Seth (2001: 330).

[13] Macedo (2000a: 1). Note that here, and in the rest of the book, 'diversity' is more or less a synonym of 'pluralism'. I prefer the use of the word 'diversity' rather than 'pluralism' because I would like to make a distinction between value pluralism (understood as a view about the nature of moral value) and pluralism

with moral, political, ethnical, religious, sexual, and social diversities. As I already stressed on giving a definition of the principal features of liberalism, diversity is not a new condition for such a political view. In this regard, Kwame A. Appiah goes still further suggesting that 'the matter of diversity, far from being marginal to the origin of modern political philosophy, was central to it.'[14] However, even narrowing the scope of our enquiry to liberalism and accepting the view that its origins are to be traced back to the search for a peaceful coexistence after the sixteenth- and seventeenth-century Wars of Religion, one cannot deny that liberalism had to do with diversity of religious, moral, and cultural beliefs since its beginning.[15] What is rather new is both the increased consciousness of this diversity and the fact that it is not immediately considered as a deviance. Some reasons for this are globalization, enhanced migration, the claims for inclusion advanced by previously excluded minorities, and the spread of a general egalitarian ethos grounded in the acceptance of the morality of human rights.

Thus, the present book discusses how liberalism deals with diversity as understood in the way just sketched. Things become quite complex when we consider the fact that diversity does not always fit easily within the boundaries drawn by liberal theory. In fact, the diversity a liberal state should deal with might be represented also by individuals and groups who reject some crucial liberal tenets, such as gender equality and freedom of conscience.[16] As the following chapters will show, challenging problems arise in considering the width of diversity that should be accommodated within the borders of a liberal society, the constraints that bind the acceptability of claims for accommodation, and whether and how diversity poses a threat to the unity and stability of the liberal polity as traditionally understood.

---

as a fact (diversity). As we will see, value pluralism is one of the foundations of William Galston's *diversity liberalism* (see Chapter 3).

[14] Appiah (2005: xv).

[15] For some accounts of historical origins of liberalism according to which Wars of Religion are the starting point of liberalism, see Larmore (1996) and Rawls (2005).

[16] Alessandro Ferrara (2014: 91) calls 'hyperpluralism' the condition that liberalism is called upon to face in the contemporary world.

Accordingly, a discussion on liberalism and diversity can be particularly relevant in the debates on regulation of the internal life of traditional (either religious or secular) communities that reject any simple assimilation to the practices of the majority society. For instance, some groups, such as the Amish, in order to preserve their integrity, may want that their children to take advantage of public education only for a limited number of years.[17]

Reflecting on liberalism and diversity can be paramount also in those cases in which a group wants that some spheres of its existence be ruled according to norms that are different from the ones imposed by the liberal framework on the rest of the society. Think, for example, about how some Muslim communities might want to regulate divorce, and the debate this had generated in India some decades ago. In this regard, one needs to refer to the so-called Shah Bano case.[18] In April 1985, the Indian Supreme Court ruled that Shah Bano, a Muslim woman unilaterally divorced by her husband, had to receive a maintenance allowance from him. Although the Indian Constitution officially recognizes the personal laws of several religious communities,[19] the Supreme Court gave its judgment on the basis of priority of the secular law, according to which indigent women should receive maintenance from their former husbands. However, Muslim personal law could recommend a different solution, which could infringe on women's rights and equality. The Supreme Court's decision was strongly contested by the Muslims, who feared being forced to yield to Hindu supremacy. Muslims felt that due to the subordination of religious personal law to secular law, their religious and cultural identity was under threat. This Supreme Court decision was nullified in 1986, when the legislature passed the Muslim Women (Protection of Rights on Divorce) Act. With this measure, the Muslims obtained recognition of the relevance of their religious personal law, since the state was forced to not intervene in their marriage and divorce affairs. However, the status of women was somehow lowered, since there was

---

[17] See Chapter 3.

[18] For a detailed discussion of the Shah Bano case, see Hasan (2005), MacKinnon (2006), Mullally (2004), and Nussbaum (2001).

[19] These communities are Muslims, Hindus, Christians, and Parsees. See Mahajan (2005b: 296). Furthermore, people are largely in support of the plurality of personal laws. See Mitra (2013).

a restriction of the period in which husbands could be liable to pay the maintenance to their past wives.

Regardless of the juridical and political details, the Shah Bano case brings to light some of the concerns that will be at the centre of this book: how much can the life of a group be governed according to rules that are in contrast with the ones that the rest of the society respects? How is the autonomy of a group to be understood from what will be here called mainstream society? What happens when, as in the Shah Bano case, there is a conflict between equality and diversity, namely, the equality guaranteed by the secular liberal democratic order and the preservation of cultural and religious diversity?[20]

With regard to such and related issues, some theorists who praise diversity experience liberal democratic political institutions and liberal theories as unfairly sectarian and blind to social pluralism. Some multiculturalists, feminists, postmodernists, and anti-liberals of various sorts have maintained that liberalism, with its classical aspirations to freedom, equality, and social unity, is unduly homogenizing towards different varieties of cultures, conceptions of the good, and forms of life that are widespread in contemporary societies. However, this effacement of social diversity is not a necessary upshot of liberalism. Contrariwise, as this book will demonstrate, liberalism (if properly understood) is the right answer to the problems created by diversity.

The charge of being culturally particularistic is another challenge liberalism has to face. As Bhikhu Parekh has written, liberalism is 'historically specific, bound to a particular culture, economy, and polity'.[21] Liberalism, critics such as Parekh say, was born in the West and cannot be detached from Western history, culture, economic, and political institutions. Thus, if all this holds, liberalism cannot aspire to be valid beyond the West. However, the liberalism defended in this book does not fall victim to this objection. As the following pages will show,[22] the theory defended in this

---

[20] The equality–diversity conflict is particularly relevant for those who are sensitive to gender issues. The preservation and defence of cultural diversity, in some cases, reinforces social hierarchies in which women are subordinated. See Mahajan (2005a), Okin (1999), Shachar (1998), and Spinner-Halev (2001).

[21] Parekh (2011: 81).

[22] See especially Chapter 5. The 'particularity' objection will be more extensively met in the section, 'The (Alleged) Cultural Particularity of Liberalism' of Chapter 7.

book has minimal commitment and is overall parsimonious. It is more a theory on the limits of the power of the government, rather than a theory on how people should behave in their daily lives. This statement, rather obscure at the moment, will be clearer after having read what follows. Now, drawing some distinctions within liberal theory is required.

Liberal Distinctions: Political and Comprehensive, Pro-autonomy and Pro-toleration

As I observed in the previous section, liberalism is a complex tradition of political thought. This complexity is reflected in the existence of many and often contrasting liberal doctrines. In this section, I attempt to put some conceptual order within the rich field of liberal theories. I give an account of two distinctions one can draw in liberalism. The first concerns the two ways in which a theory can be justified, whereas the other pertains to two different principles a theory can assume as fundamental. Combining these two distinctions, I obtain four theories. This conceptualization offers a fairly complete map of the available liberal positions, among which I will select the one that deals with diversity in the most appropriate way.

If one considers how a liberal theory is justified, one can have *political* or *comprehensive* liberalism. Liberalism understood as a comprehensive doctrine[23] is defended by John Locke, Immanuel Kant, and John Stuart Mill. In spite of the differences between their theories, all share the following feature: '[T]hey relate liberal commitments in political philosophy to some vision or conception of what matters in life and of the human person and its place in the world.'[24] These accounts of liberalism do not hide the fact that their liberal commitment is grounded in a wide account of human flourishing, or in theories about moral value, metaphysics, and religion. Comprehensive liberals maintain that political theory cannot eschew references to substantive moral or metaphysical normative

---

[23] As Samuel Freeman (2007: 332) writes in a monograph on Rawls, '[A] comprehensive doctrine includes what is of value in life and gives life its meaning. Metaphysical doctrines regarding the nature of reality, and epistemological doctrines regarding the possibility and conditions of human knowledge are also comprehensive doctrines, as are all religions.'

[24] Waldron (2004: 91).

considerations. It is in such deep commitments that comprehensive liberals ground the defence of traditional liberal concerns, such as the respect of individual rights, neutrality, and toleration. For instance, as Charles Larmore writes, 'Kant and Mill sought to justify the principle of neutrality by appealing to the ideals of autonomy and individuality',[25] while Will Kymlicka, a contemporary comprehensive liberal, defends toleration based on the value of individual autonomy.[26]

Political liberalism is a recent presence in the liberal landscape. It is the view mainly elaborated by the late John Rawls in a series of articles published in the 1980s, and later systematized in his book, *Political Liberalism*.[27] In this book, Rawls develops a liberal theory understood as a *political* conception. It has three essential features: it only applies to the basic structure of society; it is independent of disputable comprehensive doctrines; and it is elaborated from ideas implicit in the culture of a liberal democratic society.[28] Nevertheless, apart from the complex details of the Rawlsian position, I will assume that 'political liberalism is not merely the name of a book by John Rawls. It is a distinctive approach to the problem of political power',[29] whose core idea is that, given the persistence of disagreement about the way in which one should live, the liberal order should not be founded on the validity of a specific comprehensive doctrine, but on what different theories can share despite their differences.

I would like to point out here that the distinction between comprehensive and political liberalism is not a difference between a moral and a non-moral political theory. A normative theory requires some moral content, and political liberalism, being a normative theory, has its own moral content. What distinguishes political from comprehensive liberalism is that the former 'tries to establish liberalism as a minimal moral conception'.[30] In plural and diverse societies, traditional liberal ideas

[25] Larmore (1990: 342). Here, 'neutrality' should be understood as the rejection of paternalistic restrictions for enforcing a specific conception of the good.

[26] Kymlicka (1995: Chapter 8). A useful discussion on Kymlicka's notion of toleration and on his reliance on autonomy can be found in Şahin (2010: Chapter 6).

[27] Rawls (2005). For the Rawlsian view of the 'politicity' of liberalism, see Maffettone (2010: Chapter 9). Other political liberals include Larmore (1990), Macedo (2000a), Moon (1993), Nussbaum (2011), and Shklar (1989).

[28] Rawls (2005: 11–15).

[29] Ackerman (2004: 79).

[30] Kukathas (2003: 17).

of autonomy and individuality (such as those defended respectively by Immanuel Kant and John Stuart Mill) are too controversial to work as the basis of a liberal democratic society. Think about traditional or religious communities who place particular emphasis on the value of group membership. As Larmore maintains, traditional liberal values, such as autonomy or individuality, 'have themselves become simply another part of the problem'.[31] Thus, political power should be exercised according to reasons and principles that everyone can accept independently of the comprehensive doctrine they endorse in their lives. Underlying political liberalism is the confidence that a liberal society can be just and stable even if individuals do not share comprehensive commitments.

The second distinction I consider here concerns the core principles of liberal theory. Autonomy and toleration are values that a liberal theory can assume as fundamental. Note, though, that this assumption of autonomy or toleration as the main tenet of a liberal theory is subordinated to the acceptance of individualism and egalitarianism in the minimal sense I specified earlier.

In *Liberal Pluralism*, William Galston talks about 'two quite different variants of liberal thought based on two distinct principles'.[32] Thus, *pro-autonomy* (or Enlightenment) and *pro-toleration* (or pro-diversity or Reformation) are the liberalisms one obtains if one thinks about the crucial liberal value. In general, pro-autonomy liberals tend to value autonomy in the sense of 'individual self-direction in at least one of the many senses explored by John Locke, Immanuel Kant, John Stuart Mill, and American writing in an Emersonian vein'.[33] Pro-autonomy theorists stress the importance of rational self-reflection, individual choice, and revisability of the conceptions of the good. Pro-toleration liberals, on the other hand, are more *diversity friendly*. In general, they tend to maximize the public space in which both individuals and groups can enact their difference, provided that social unity is protected.[34] Furthermore, pro-toleration liberalism supporters advance the view that liberalism is not a theory necessarily committed to the (although not coercive) promotion of

---

[31] Larmore (1990: 345).
[32] Galston (2002a: 20).
[33] Galston (2002a: 21).
[34] See Galston (1995: 524).

autonomous lifestyles. For them, human life can flourish in several, and not necessarily autonomy-oriented, ways.

Jacob T. Levy has tried to locate the above-mentioned distinction within the history of political thought. In fact, he claims that 'the autonomy/toleration dispute is not a new one, but one as old as liberalism itself'.[35] The distinction is rephrased as one between rationalist and pluralist liberalism. Rationalist liberals (Kant, Mill, and Voltaire) are committed to 'intellectual progress, universalism, and equality before a unified law, opposed to arbitrary and irrational distinctions and inequalities, and determined to disrupt local tyrannies'. Pluralist liberals (Acton, Montesquieu, and Tocqueville) are 'hostile to the central state and friendly toward local, customary, voluntary, or intermediate bodies, communities, and associations'.[36] Both rationalists and pluralists share a common commitment to the recognition of the value of political freedoms, but they have different attitudes towards the relation between individuals and communities. Rationalist liberals are generally more suspicious than pluralists about the dangers represented by intra-group oppression. However, membership in one of the two liberal traditions does not forestall possibilities of sharing concerns with the other tradition. For instance, a liberal rationalist will admit limits to the promotion of autonomy, whereas a liberal pluralist will recognize that group authority comes to an end in cases of gross violation of human rights.

Combining the two distinctions I am considering (see Table 1.1 for a graphic representation), I obtain four kinds of liberal theories: comprehensive pro-autonomy (hereafter CA); comprehensive pro-toleration (hereafter CT); political pro-autonomy (hereafter PA); and political pro-toleration (hereafter PT). In this way, one achieves a wide overview of possible liberalisms. This list, since there might be other forms of liberalism beyond the four considered here, is not exhaustive. However, as it will be clear later, this framework is helpful in understanding the contemporary debate about liberalism and diversity.

In addition, this way of attempting to systematize the plurality of liberal theories is significantly more fine-grained than the one assumed in much recent political philosophy. For example, discussing whether autonomy or toleration is the fundamental liberal principle, Will

---

[35] Levy (2003: 281).
[36] Levy (2003: 279).

TABLE 1.1   The Plurality of Liberal Theories

	Fundamental value	
Justification	Autonomy	Toleration
Political	PA	PT
Comprehensive	CA	CT

Source: Compiled by author.

Kymlicka writes: '[T]his contrast is described in different ways—e.g. a contrast between "comprehensive" and "political" liberalism, or between "Enlightenment" or "Reformation" liberalism.'[37] I think that Kymlicka simply conflates a distinction about justificatory procedures ('political' or 'comprehensive') with one about liberalism's fundamental value ('autonomy' or 'toleration'). In his framework, any comprehensive liberalism is ipso facto pro-autonomy, whereas any political liberalism is ipso facto pro-diversity. The outcome of this conflation is an impoverished account of the richness of the available liberal positions. Indeed, as the following pages will show, a political liberalism can be both pro-autonomy and pro-toleration, while a comprehensive liberalism can be both pro-autonomy and pro-toleration.

Plan of the Work

The book proceeds as follows. Chapters 2–5 illustrate one of the possible liberal positions. These positions, namely, CA liberalism, CT liberalism, PA liberalism, and PT liberalism, will not be considered in abstract terms but will be exemplified through the work of some influential liberal theorists. A tight analysis of CA liberalism, CT liberalism, and PA liberalism demonstrates that they present some weaknesses that make them seriously defective. At the end of the analysis of the competing accounts, a specific form of PT liberalism will emerge as my favourite theoretical position. This is then followed by two more chapters. In Chapter 6, I compare PT liberalism with the issue of religious pluralism in India, and prove that it is preferable to some prominent Indian accounts. Finally,

---

[37] Kymlicka (2002: 229).

in Chapter 7, I recapitulate the argument of the book and defend it from some possible objections.

Proceeding in order, in Chapters 2 and 3, I discuss and criticize comprehensive liberalisms' attempt to accommodate diversity. Comprehensive pro-autonomy liberalism will be illustrated in Chapter 2 through the exposition of Will Kymlicka's theory. Kymlicka works out a systematic liberal theory sensitive to cultural belonging and minority rights. The liberalism he defends is overtly comprehensive and pro-autonomy, and alleges to be adequate in addressing the cultural diversity represented by national and ethnic minorities (or migrants). Kymlicka maintains that one needs an appeal to the value of individual autonomy for protecting and enforcing the whole range of liberal rights and freedoms. The same appeal to individual autonomy is required in order to justify the rights liberalism is requested to grant to minorities. Kymlicka understands autonomy mainly as rational revisability of ends. In his argument, choice has value only as far as the condition that makes possible to individuate what is valuable. In this sense, Kymlicka's notion of choice and autonomy is less substantive than those of Kant (according to which choice is intrinsically valuable as it reflects human rational nature) and Mill (which appeals to the intrinsic value of individuality).[38]

However, in spite of caution in the use of the notion of autonomy, it is exactly the reliance on this value that make Kymlicka's CA liberalism seriously defective as far as the accommodation of diversity is considered. In fact, Kymlicka explicitly aims at *liberalizing* (that is, making them more liberal, in the sense of more autonomy-oriented) the minorities. Under this conception, even those groups who reject autonomy and whose members wish to live their lives following traditional conceptions of human flourishing should be liberalized. The liberalization in question might transform minorities into something they reject as extraneous to their conception of the good life. Thus, the liberalization of minorities puts their diversity at risk and entails disrespect for their conception of the good. This means that our search for a theory that is able to accommodate diversity should go beyond CA liberalism.

Chapter 3 engages with William Galston's work as an instance of CT liberalism. In this approach, a pro-diversity attitude coexists with a reliance

---

[38] See Note 7.

on comprehensive commitments (especially value pluralism[39]). Galston's diversity liberalism promises to be more accommodating of diversity than CA liberalism. He objects to any version of autonomy liberalism on the basis that autonomy is not the only possible and legitimate way of life in liberal societies. This strategy overtly points towards an extended acceptance of diversity. In fact, Galston states that if public institutions assume autonomy's primacy, individuals and groups who deny that autonomy is always required for human thriving could experience alienation in the liberal public space. As one can easily note, in our societies, there are many individuals and groups whose ideal of human flourishing is in no way associated with autonomous choice, critical self-reflection, and all those attitudes generally related with a liberal–rationalistic idea of individual. Thus, according to Galston, 'properly understood, liberalism is about the protection of diversity, not the valorisation of choice.'[40] Assuming the protection of diversity as the core value of a political theory allows Galston's theory to pursue 'a policy of *maximum feasible accommodation*',[41] constrained by the requisites of civic unity and individual security. Moreover, such an assumption enables political institutions to take diversity seriously, without imposing liberal values on those groups that live in contemporary liberal societies and still do not accept the primacy of liberal and autonomy-oriented ideals of human thriving.

In the final part of Chapter 3, I raise a series of objections that show inadequacies in Galston's theory. I focus especially on the way in which Galston makes use of value pluralism. My point is that, contrary to the author's explicit intentions and to the nature of value pluralism itself, Galston's view of value pluralism might lead towards ethical relativism. Further problems for Galston's view come both from his assumption of diversity as a value to be protected, rather than a merely factual condition to be faced, and from his strong conception of exit rights.

After the rejection of comprehensive liberalism, both in its pro-autonomy and pro-toleration versions, Chapter 4 gives an account of PA liberalism. It is a theory that combines the politicization of liberalism with a

---

[39] Roughly, value pluralism is the view according to which there are many moral values that can clash among themselves. For further details, see the discussion in Chapter 3.

[40] Galston (1991: 329).

[41] Galston (2002a: 20).

commitment to autonomy (although, as I explain, this is a *political* notion of autonomy). The politicization is introduced with the aim of improving comprehensive liberalism's capacity to grasp and accommodate the fact of diversity. In fact, as Stephen Macedo (whose work is assumed as a relevant example of PA liberalism) maintains, political liberalism should be preferred because it accommodates greater diversity at the foundational level than comprehensive liberalism. Political liberalism does not rely on the validity of one among many conflicting conceptions of the good. For this reason, it can fairly accommodate and acknowledge the persistent disagreement concerning the ultimate matters of ethics, religion, and philosophy. Yet, this liberal theory does not stand for a passive and undiscriminating acceptance of diversity. There are 'healthy' and 'unhealthy' forms of diversity, and there is a need to distinguish among those that can be accommodated and others that should be rejected or somehow constrained or contained.

As a matter of fact, Macedo's liberalism is very demanding. According to him, liberal societies rely on 'shared political commitments' and on 'a shared public morality',[42] rather than on mere diversity. In order to perpetuate a liberal society, specific citizens' virtues are needed. However, these virtues cannot be generated by themselves. This is the reason why substantive public intervention (primarily through the system of public education) is required. Another central aspect that highlights the demanding nature of PA liberalism consists in the fact that it aims at encouraging people to become *politically* autonomous, that is, autonomous as free and equal citizens in a liberal democratic regime. This latter requirement, as Chapter 4 will clarify, is somehow puzzling since it blurs the distinction between political and comprehensive liberalism in practical terms.

The most serious problems for PA liberalism, however, arise in its approach to the accommodation of diversity, as well as in its conceptualization of the majority–minorities relationships in the process of inclusion of the latter. Political pro-autonomy liberalism claims that diversity needs to be transformed to become supportive of the liberal order. In this process of transformation, the primacy of majority is so strong that the task of establishing the terms of inclusion (or even assimilation) of minorities within the liberal domain rests only on them. However, as I

---

[42] Macedo (2000a: 146).

contend in the text, these transformations do not adequately consider the voice and the status of the minorities.

Thus, Chapter 4 rejects PA liberalism despite the fact that politicization is a promising move in the effort to remedy the faults of comprehensive liberalism. Indeed, as I argue in the following chapter, the political turn should be completed with a commitment to diversity rather than to autonomy. Political pro-toleration liberalism, in fact, combines the politicization of liberalism with a general pro-diversity orientation.

In Chapter 5, the work of Chandran Kukathas[43] is considered as a relevant example of the principles of PT liberalism. The commitment to toleration in Kukathas's theory is grounded in the value of freedom of conscience, and is so strong that any primacy to individual autonomy is challenged. Further, and this shows the political character of Kukathas's theory, liberalism is seen not as a theory that should aim at justice, but at fixing the common terms of peaceful coexistence in societies marked by deep and pervasive disagreements with regard to culture, ethics, religion, and so on.[44] For Kukathas, a genuine liberal society is 'an archipelago of different communities operating in a sea of mutual toleration'.[45] It is, in other terms, an association of associations enjoying an extensive degree of reciprocal autonomy. In this picture, the role of the state is severely restrained, since its functions are limited to the guarantee of peace and to the maintenance of social order.

Although the liberal archipelago is a promising starting point in the definition of PT liberalism, Kukathas's view is strongly criticized in Chapter 5. It actually becomes acceptable only after some substantial amendments. I argue that Kukathas's approach misrepresents the relations of individuals with groups and mainstream society.[46] Further, after

---

[43] Kukathas (2003).

[44] Ensuring peace under conditions of diversity is the main goal pursued by PT liberalism. Note that PT liberalism aims at peaceful coexistence of groups regardless of the achievement of justice. Aiming at a just society, especially through the imposition of equality or the recognition of group claims, can nurture existing conflicts, or even engender opportunities for new conflicts. For more on this point, see Chapters 5 and 6.

[45] Kukathas (2003: 8).

[46] By 'mainstream society', as Chapter 5 will clarify, I mean 'political community' or 'political society', namely, the common social space inhabited by individuals independently from the group to which they belong.

an enquiry into the kind of obligations binding individuals to groups and to the mainstream society (and to the state[47]), I claim that understanding such obligations as associative obligations can render PT liberalism more tenable. This view is increasingly defensible when it is completed with a much more extended account of the mainstream society. Furthermore, this mainstream society is required to give effectiveness to those exit rights that, as I will prove in the chapter, play a crucial role in Kukathas's liberalism. Thus, a properly conceived PT liberalism (which is the position I defend) has to find place for a unitary central state despite Kukathas's anarchical sympathies.

The functions of the state ought to be consistent with the view that what matters more is the safeguard of a peaceful coexistence under conditions of deep diversity. Thus, a state constrained by the framework offered by PT liberalism will end up having the following duties: it has to prevent inter-groups exploitation; it has to aim at making the mainstream society responsive to the needs of all the individuals; and it has to defend individuals from the violation of fundamental rights both within and outside the groups to which they belong.

Chapter 6, in a way, tests the practical import of PT liberalism. In this chapter, by some means, I take the *spirit* of a suggestion by Rajeev Bhargava. He writes that 'aspiring political philosophers anywhere in the world must take a crash course in Indian politics, society, and culture.'[48] In fact, India is a paradigmatic example of diversity along all the relevant dimensions considered in this book. Thus, any theory aiming at dealing with issues such as the ones entailed by the accommodation of diversity should consider India as a test case to examine whether its principles make any sense in the real word.

In fact, Chapter 6 tests PT liberalism in relation to Indian religious pluralism. My idea is that if liberalism shows good resources to face such a terrific diversity, it will work as well in more simple milieus. After considering some relevant features of religious pluralism in the Indian context, I present two of the most influential theories that have tried to accommodate it.[49] These views, despite their merits in trying to defend

---

[47] The state here is seen as the institutional expression of the political community.

[48] Bhargava (2008: 3).

[49] Bhargava (1998a, 1998b) and Chandhoke (1999).

a specifically Indian understanding of secularism, are quite demanding and criticizable. The notion of equality they employ is too substantive. Indeed, this egalitarian impulse pushes the role of the state well beyond what PT liberalism requires. The problem is that the effects of the expansion of the state's powers have not always been conducive to social peace. Thus, the constraints imposed by PT liberalism to the exercise of state power are particularly required in this discourse on secularism. This is why, as far as religious pluralism in India is concerned, PT liberalism is preferable to some influential *local* proposals.

To conclude, Chapter 7 recapitulates the main arguments of the book. In this conclusive chapter, I also give an answer to the objection according to which the historical origins of liberalism are an obstacle to the acceptance of this doctrine beyond the West. Finally, I spend a few words on some topics neglected by the book. In particular, I focus on the institutional arrangements and on the account of distributive justice required by PT liberalism.

Liberalism and Minority Rights

Liberalizing Minorities

In this chapter, I will discuss comprehensive pro-autonomy liberalism (CA liberalism). In this form of liberalism, a comprehensive account of moral value coexists with a commitment to autonomy. I will illustrate CA liberalism through an exposition of Will Kymlicka's views. He works out a systematic liberal theory whose main aim is to give an account of cultural belonging and minority rights[1] consistent with his interpretation of liberal egalitarian principles. As Rajeev Bhargava has pointed out, Kymlicka's approach is a form of liberal multiculturalism: it is 'liberal because equal recognition of cultural groups must be compatible with requirements of basic individual liberties'.[2] In this sense, liberal multiculturalism is significantly different from those authoritarian forms of multiculturalism that, attaching value only to identity, culture, and belonging, acknowledge the equal value of all groups, even the ones who override basic individual liberties. Liberal multiculturalism, as this chapter will show, holds individual liberty, autonomy, identity, and belonging in high regard, but will end up being particularly troublesome. In fact,

---

[1] The minorities Kymlicka is talking about are *cultural* minorities. The meaning of 'culture' will be clarified in this chapter.

[2] Bhargava (2010: 109–10).

despite the acknowledgement of the value of groups and cultural belonging, it 'tilts in favour of individual autonomy'.[3]

In the next section, I will briefly discuss some of the issues liberalism
has had to face, especially with regard to the notion of citizenship, as a
consequence of the emerging moral, political, and cultural differences
that have made an appearance in the last few decades. Then, after a presentation of Kymlicka's liberalism and of the ways in which it assigns
value to cultural membership, I will account for the place of minority
rights within CA liberalism. The focus of the following section will be
on the consistency of liberalism with minority rights. The last two sections will present some objections to CA liberalism, arising both from its
reliance on autonomy and from the fact that it misconceives the actual
character of diversity represented by immigrants.

Liberalism and Differentiated Citizenship

The diffusion in both political philosophy and public debate of terms
such as 'multiculturalism', 'politics of difference', 'politics of identity',
and 'politics of recognition' signals the crisis of the model of citizenship
founded on the possession of universal and common individual rights.[4]
This model, predominant in liberal democratic countries since the second post-War period, granted the recognition of the status of citizen to
all the individuals belonging to a state by conceding social and political
rights. Possession of the rights of citizenship, however, did not prevent
some groups (for example, blacks, gays and lesbians, women, religious
minorities, immigrants, and indigenous people) from being and feeling
marginalized, oppressed, or excluded. In fact, as Kymlicka contends,
'many groups feel marginalized and stigmatized despite the possession
of common rights of citizenship. Many members of these groups feel
marginalized, not (or not only) because of their socio-economic status,
but also because of their socio-cultural identity—their "difference".'[5]

The practice of differentiating citizens by sociocultural identity has
seemed necessary in order to stem the exclusion of minorities, and to

---

[3] Bhargava (2010: 121).
[4] See Marshall (1965).
[5] Kymlicka (2002: 239).

ensure that the deep diversity and cultural pluralism that characterize modern Western societies were accepted, recognized, and accommodated. Traditionally, in fact, differences were obscured by a sense of citizenship that assumed a model of the individual (usually male, white, and heterosexual) as universal, which, in reality, is far from it. Requests for acceptance, recognition, and accommodation have been often made by people considered not as isolated individuals but as members of excluded or oppressed groups. Therefore, the process of developing an idea of citizenship more sensitive to the diversity represented by minorities has led to the emergence of controversial concepts such as 'collective rights' or 'group rights'.

Liberalism, being an individualistic political theory, has been seen by many critics as unable to articulate an effective defence of minority rights. In fact, until at least the late 1980s, the discourse on minority rights was perceived as a general reaction to the individualistic abstraction and atomism of contemporary liberalism.[6] The liberal emphasis on individual autonomy and on moral individualism has been taken, for instance, by communitarian theorists,[7] as a proof that liberalism cannot account for the social nature of the individual and consequently, for the rights of minorities. For these reasons, Bhargava claims, the discourse on multiculturalism and on the accommodation of diversity represents 'a large intellectual move away from the mainstream tradition of enlightenment political philosophy'.[8]

However, as the following text will show, Kymlicka's theoretical work tries to exceed the alleged narrowness of liberal individualism and, at the same time, introduces noteworthy elements of discontinuity within the domain of liberal theories. Kymlicka's project is, indeed, to locate the discourse on cultural pluralism within liberalism and to 'justify minority rights as a means of protecting distinctive cultural communities, the survival of which is deemed vital to the freedom and equality of their individual members'.[9]

---

[6] Kymlicka (2001a: 18).

[7] As examples of communitarian thinkers, one can consider at least Michael Sandel and Alasdair MacIntyre. See MacIntyre (1984) and Sandel (1982).

[8] Bhargava (2010: 103).

[9] Murphy (2012: 62–3).

Liberalism and Cultural Membership

Kymlicka conceives liberalism 'as a normative political philosophy, a set of moral arguments about the justification of political actions and institutions'.[10] Liberalism is distinguished by its recognition of fundamental freedoms for individuals and for enabling everyone to choose and freely rework their conceptions of the good.

Kymlicka takes the following statement as his point of departure for the analysis of the political morality of liberalism: 'our essential interest is in leading a good life, in having those things that a good life contains.'[11] This assertion should not be interpreted in the relativistic or sceptical sense, according to which all lives have value regardless of the values someone endorses. In fact, Kymlicka claims that 'leading a good life is different from leading the life we *currently believe* to be good.'[12] Human beings are fallible and can foster false beliefs about the value of what they are pursuing. The deliberative process to identify which life is good and which values should be pursued does not take place in a vacuum but in a social context in which interdependence among people holds. Actually, it is in this very context that people find valuable and worthless options they have to choose or reject in order to give a meaning to their lives.

Even from these brief remarks, one might raise doubts on the strength of the objections according to which liberalism is based on the idea of a person divorced from social relations, whose interests and preferences are given regardless of social conditioning. John Stuart Mill and John Rawls, along with Ronald Dworkin, are the liberal authors who have most influenced the theoretical work of Kymlicka. All these thinkers did

---

[10] Kymlicka (1989a: 9).

[11] Kymlicka (1989a: 10). The philosophical status of this and of the other two propositions that, as will be shown, constitute the political morality of liberalism is not clear. As Bhikhu Parekh (2006: 105) has observed: Kymlicka 'sometimes says that [the three propositions] represent basic liberal beliefs; at other times he takes them to be general truths about human life and argues or implies that, because liberalism is based on them, it is truer or rationally more defensible than other political doctrines.' In the first case, the three propositions would be relevant only for individuals who already are liberal. In the second case, it should be showed that the propositions are convincing; instead, as we will see later, it is possible to raise doubts about their acceptability.

[12] Kymlicka (1989a: 10).

not take the idea of an atomistically conceived moral subject as the cornerstone of their liberalism. Contrariwise, they insisted that individual conceptions of the good are formed in society and that the character is shaped and changed in many ways by social interaction.[13]

Kymlicka's exposition of the morality of liberalism is completed by two other propositions that are preconditions for the realization of the good life: '[O]ne is that we lead our life from the inside, in accordance with our beliefs about what gives value to life; the other is that we be free to question those beliefs, to examine them in the light of whatever information and examples our culture can provide.'[14] Something is valuable for an individual only when s/he endorses it. For instance, a religious belief is not valuable when it is coercively imposed and is not the outcome of a free process of deliberation. It is from these considerations that, according to Kymlicka, are derived those civic and personal liberties that have been traditionally associated with liberalism, as well as the aversion to unjustified paternalism and an interest in the protection of privacy. Moreover, human fallibility must be acknowledged, in that every person should be able to live in an environment that allows her/him to know different conceptions of the good and to have the information necessary to examine her/his life plan and review it as needed. From these additional considerations, one can recognize the centrality of the state in the education of citizens and the importance of other individual freedoms dear to liberalism, such as the freedoms of expression, association, and the press.

Thus, a liberalism such as Kymlicka's is not abstractly individualistic. Moreover, it recognizes the fundamental relevance of culture and cultural membership. In fact, despite the claim that in a liberal society it is ultimately the individual who decides how s/he should live, Kymlicka acknowledges that 'this decision is always a matter of selecting what we believe to be most valuable from the various options available, selecting from a context of choice which provides us with different ways of life.'[15] Individuals choose among the options that their culture makes available to them. So, for Kymlicka, culture is primarily the context within which

---

[13] To strengthen his thesis, Kymlicka quotes John Rawls, from Rawls (1999a: 240), and John Stuart Mill, from Leavis (1962: 71). See Kymlicka (1989a: 14–16).

[14] Kymlicka (1989a: 13).

[15] Kymlicka (1989a: 164).

individuals choose how to give meaning to their lives.[16] For this reason, liberalism attributes value to a culture not for itself but because it is the context within which individual choices take place and acquire meaning.

Culture is essential for individuals in a second sense: it gives them identity. The members of a culture tend to identify with it to the point that even their self-respect is influenced by how their culture is perceived by others. In other words, 'if a culture is not generally respected, then the dignity and self respect of its members will also be threatened.'[17] Kymlicka specifies that the value of cultural membership does not concern only traditional societies but also liberal societies in which freedom and individual rights are protected and there is no conception of the good shared by all citizens. In this sense, the liberal approach to cultural membership differs from the communitarian one, which presupposes that individuals are constitutively linked to a community that shares a particular conception of the good.

At this point, it should be noted that when Kymlicka talks about cultures, he refers to 'societal cultures' insofar as he wants to emphasize that they concern not only those memories and values that people share but also the political institutions and practices regulating common life. More precisely, according to Kymlicka, a societal culture 'is a culture territorially concentrated, based on a shared language that is used in many social institutions, both in public and private (schools, media, law, economics, government)'. It 'requires a language and common institutions, rather than common religious beliefs, family habits, personal lifestyles'.[18] This means that a societal culture can be (and in liberal settlements, usually is) pluralistic. The creation of cultures understood along these lines is a social phenomenon primarily related to the process of modernization. Kymlicka claims that 'modernization involves the diffusion throughout a society of a common culture, including a standardized language, embodied in common economic, political, and educational institutions.'[19] The existence of societal cultures, as Kymlicka understands them, was instrumental in the development of the modern economy, and has made possible the spread of the high level of solidarity needed to support the

---

[16] Kymlicka (1995: 82–4).
[17] Kymlicka (1995: 89).
[18] Kymlicka (2001a: 25).
[19] Kymlicka (1995: 76).

mechanisms of the welfare state. Furthermore, the existence of a public education system has allowed the emergence of the notion of equality of opportunity, which is one of the foundations of the democratic system.

Cultural Pluralism and Minority Rights

In *Multicultural Citizenship*, Kymlicka distinguishes between two types of cultural diversity to which two types of state correspond. In the first case, 'cultural diversity arises from the incorporation of previously self-govern-ing, territorially concentrated cultures into a larger state.'[20] This incorpo-ration can concern both indigenous peoples and groups who continue to perceive themselves as authentic nations within a larger state[21] even after colonization or conquest. Cultures that are incorporated are called 'national minorities', whereas the state in which there are national minorities is called 'multinational'. In a multinational state, therefore, there are two or more distinct societal cultures, and minority cultures do not aspire to assimila-tion, but to a form of autonomy or self-government that enables them to preserve their cultural identity. The United States of America (USA) and Canada are considered examples of multinational states. In USA, national minorities are represented by Puerto Ricans, Native American tribes, Aboriginal Hawaiians, and all those groups who have been involuntarily annexed as a result of conquest or colonization. The Canadian national minorities are represented by Aborigines and the people of Quebec.

Immigration represents the second form of cultural diversity. Groups of immigrants are called ethnic groups, whereas a state in which there are immigrants is called 'polyethnic'. Immigrants do not have a societal culture distinct from the majority culture. In fact, Kymlicka believes that immigrants, having voluntarily transferred to another state, are willing to integrate into the new society without claiming to reconstitute their original societal culture[22] in the country where they have moved. A state may be both multinational and polyethnic, like USA and Canada, where there are both national minorities and immigrant communities.

---

[20] Kymlicka (1995: 10).

[21] Those groups are called 'substate national groups'. See Kymlicka (2007c: 68).

[22] As will be seen later, immigrants lack the possibility of constructing their societal culture into their host society.

Kymlicka notes (and welcomes) that in recent years, there has been a general acceptance of policies in favour of cultural minorities and of multiculturalism, conceived as accommodation of cultural diversity, in many Western democracies. In his last monograph on multiculturalism, Kymlicka identifies three principles underpinning the spread of multiculturalism. First, there is the abandonment of the view that the state is the sole property of the dominant cultural group in favour of the view that 'the State must be considered as belonging to all citizens equally.'[23] Second, one can see the gradual diffusion and acceptance of the idea that minorities should not be coercively assimilated or excluded, but that they can participate in the public sphere as equals and can assert without discrimination their ethnic identities. Finally, there has been the recognition of wrongs committed by majorities against minorities, and the acceptance of the legitimacy of compensatory policies.

In *Multicultural Citizenship*, Kymlicka categorizes the measures taken by multinational or polyethnic states to accommodate cultural diversity.[24] Kymlicka distinguishes between self-government rights, polyethnic rights, and special representation rights. Self-government rights concern political autonomy or territorial jurisdiction granted to national minorities. Polyethnic rights are those rights granted to immigrants and religious minorities to express their cultural particularities (for example, the financing of some cultural activities of the minorities and exemptions from laws that disproportionately impact certain groups). Finally, special representation rights are rights designed to cover the deficit of representativeness in political institutions with regard to expectations and interests of minorities.

All these kinds of rights constitute 'forms of group-differentiated citizenship'[25] because they are attributed not to the individual as such, but to the individual considered as member of a cultural group. In these cases, often people talk about collective rights, suggesting a 'false dichotomy'[26] with individual rights, as if all group-differentiated rights were collectively

---

[23] Kymlicka (2007c: 65). See also Kymlicka (2007a: 18–19).
[24] Kymlicka (1995: 27). In Kymlicka (2007c: 66–7), there is a detailed list of policies adopted by multicultural states in the attempt to accommodate cultural minorities.
[25] Kymlicka (1995: 45).
[26] Kymlicka (1995: 45).

exercised. Instead, as Kymlicka observes, there are some rights that are attributed to groups but are exercised by individuals, for example, the right to use the language of a minority cultural group. What does matter, however, is not whether individuals or collectivities exercise such rights but the reasons 'why the members of some [groups] should have rights regarding land, language, representation, etc. that the members of other groups do not have'.[27]

In the next section, I will show that the reasons for granting these rights are, as Kymlicka says, consistent with liberal principles. Indeed, the acknowledgement of the legitimacy of these measures, Kymlicka claims, is entailed by these very principles. Sensitiveness to the cultural context is not extraneous to liberal tradition,[28] but has been, nevertheless, undervalued by contemporary liberal theorists such as John Rawls and Ronald Dworkin. The latter have put social pluralism at the centre of their theoretical work, but nonetheless have misunderstood the real nature of cultural diversity. In fact, they have mistakenly assumed that each country has a unique (although plural) societal culture. Thus, they have only considered the pluralism that is internal to a societal culture, and have neglected the possible existence of more than one societal culture within a single national polity.[29]

Minority Rights and Liberalism

Kymlicka claims that 'the basic principles of liberalism are principles of individual freedom' and that minority rights can be acceptable from a liberal point of view only when 'they are consistent with respect for the freedom or autonomy of individuals'.[30] Minority rights are to be seen as measures to protect a culture,[31] and in order to argue that these rights are

---

[27] Kymlicka (1995: 46).

[28] Kymlicka (1989a: Chapter X, 1995: Chapter IV).

[29] Kymlicka (1995: 77).

[30] Kymlicka (1995: 75).

[31] When Kymlicka talks about the protection of a culture, he does not mean the protection of the *character* of a culture (namely, those norms, values, and institutions that are widespread in a community at a certain time) but the defence of the cultural *structure*, namely, of culture as a context of choice. In this sense, 'the cultural community continues to exist even when its members are free to modify

consistent with the principles of liberalism, it is necessary to show that the defence of a culture can be a source of legitimate claims by individuals.

The underlying idea is that the liberal nation-state has failed in its attempt to conceal difference within its borders in order to create a homogeneous society. Contrariwise, one can observe the emergence of the view that 'the liberal nation-state must acknowledge the reality of diversity and take the necessary steps to create not only an economically—but also a culturally—just society.'[32] Kymlicka claims that minority rights, understood as claims consistent with liberalism, are the proper solution to this problem. It is significant that in the last few years, Kymlicka has stressed the link between multicultural provision of minority rights and human rights. He understands the general phenomenon of multiculturalism as 'part of a larger human rights revolution involving ethnic and racial diversity'.[33] This means that, according to Kymlicka, the so-called human rights revolution after the Second World War provides the framework within which multicultural theory and policies have to be discussed. More specifically, human rights play two distinct and fundamental roles: they work both as source and constraint of multiculturalism. In fact, the human rights discourse, with its liberalizing effects, encourages minorities to argue in favour of the recognition of their difference. At the same time, human rights discourse limits what minorities can claim.

This twofold role of human rights will be clearer with the presentation of Kymlicka's two arguments in support of the idea of compatibility between minority rights and liberalism. The first refers to culture as the context within which individual autonomy is exercised and acquires meaning, whereas the second rests on the egalitarian grounds of liberal theory.

The first argument has been briefly discussed in an earlier section of this chapter, 'Liberalism and Cultural Membership'.[34] Individuals make choices from the options available to them within the cultural context in which they live. Thus, the culture to which they belong turns out to

---

the character of the culture, should they find its traditional ways of life no longer worthwhile.' See Kymlicka (1989a: 166–7).

[32] Şahin (2010: 89).

[33] Kymlicka (2012: 5).

[34] For further consideration, and for something more about how Kymlicka traces this argument in Ronald Dworkin's views, see Kymlicka (2004: 113–34).

be the place where individuals exercise their capacities of choosing and becoming autonomous persons. If culture is so relevant for the life of an individual, the fact that liberalism takes interest in it should not be seen as something weird or extraneous to its tradition. In fact, the interest for culture would be the interest for the conditions in which individual autonomy, one of the cornerstones of the liberal thought, flourishes.

From Kymlicka's viewpoint, for instance, the granting of rights of self-government to national minorities should be seen as a way to ensure that each individual can continue to live in the societal culture in which s/he has been nurtured and where s/he has the opportunity to choose what is valuable to her/him, in the lights of her/his own culture. Analogously, polyethnic rights are the rights that immigrants need for maintaining some aspects of their original culture when they move to another place. Thus, minority rights are measures required to ensure that individuals are granted their cultures, namely, the conditions necessary for the flourishing of her/his own individual autonomy. If this holds, there is no reason why liberalism should be suspicious or doubtful with regard to such policies in favour of cultural minorities.

At this point, a possible objection could be raised by those who point out the danger that would result from the granting to illiberal minorities of rights of the kind that we are discussing here. In such a case, minority rights might enable the oppression of individuals within an illiberal group. Kymlicka responds by making a distinction between two types of claims that a minority culture can make: internal restrictions and external protections. The first consists of those measures that a group adopts to reduce, through restriction of individual freedoms, the impact of internal dissent. This type of limitation on freedom is incompatible with liberalism and with the human rights revolution as the inspiring force of the multicultural turn. The second type, external protections, is represented by those measures that an ethnic or national group might claim to need with the aim of protecting 'its distinct existence and identity by limiting the impact of decisions of the larger society'.[35] Thus, for Kymlicka,

---

[35] Kymlicka (1995: 36). To tell the truth, the distinction between external protections and internal restrictions is not always clear. As Daniel M. Weinstock (2007: 247) has written, '[M]ost measures that groups will promulgate in order to protect themselves have both an internal and an external dimension.' For instance, the decision of a minority cultural group to protect its language by using

minority rights are acceptable when they occur in the form of external protections. In this case, there are no violations of individual rights, as long as the demand for particular forms of legal protection arises from the need to defend a minority cultural group from those decisions of the majority that could adversely affect its preservation.

The acceptability of external protection is more clear in light of the second argument of Kymlicka in favour of the compatibility between minority rights and liberalism, the one based on the egalitarian thrust of liberal theory. Both John Rawls and Ronald Dworkin's theories of distributive justice claim that we must compensate for or remove those disadvantages that, although created by morally arbitrary characteristics,[36] have a pervasive influence on the lives of individuals. In particular, Dworkin has developed a theory of justice in which the distribution of resources must be 'ambitions sensitive' and 'endowment insensitive'.[37] According to the principles of this theory, the condition of each individual should primarily be the result of her/his choices, rather than of natural or social circumstances for which s/he is not responsible.

Kymlicka thinks that the rights of cultural minorities can legitimately find a place within a theory of this sort. He argues that 'the members of minority cultures can face inequalities which are the product of their circumstances or endowment, not their choices and ambitions',[38] and that the rights of minorities can be seen as the appropriate means of countering these inequalities. Culture is a fundamental good for everyone because, as we have seen, it is the context within which individual choices take place and acquire meaning. So, the disadvantage that an individual suffers when her/his culture is in danger is particularly important and certainly does not depend on her/his decisions. Being a member of a particularly disadvantaged cultural group has to do with fate rather than with a conscious decision. Thus, the recognition of a right can 'help rectify this disadvantage, by alleviating the vulnerability of minority cultures

---

it in schools can be interpreted both as an external protection (the minority language is shielded from the impact of the majority language) and as an internal restriction (educational choices are constrained).

[36] Rawls (1999a: 14).

[37] Dworkin (2000: Chapter 2).

[38] Kymlicka (1989a: 190).

to majority decisions' and ensuring that 'members of the minority have the same opportunity to live and work in their own culture as members of the majority'.[39]

In the case of national minorities, equality allows the granting of liberal rights of self-government, by means of which a minority can keep its culture alive: 'this ensures that the good of cultural membership is equally protected for the members of all national groups.'[40]

The discourse about ethnic minorities, that is, immigrants, is different. Immigrants, as has been said earlier, do not represent separated social cultures within the majority culture. They are deprived of the necessary conditions to maintain a distinct societal culture within the state in which they move. For a societal culture to exist and flourish in the modern world requires that (within a certain territory that is territorially defined and institutionally organized) the cultural group should have 'substantial powers about language, education, public employment, and immigration'.[41] In the case of immigrants, these conditions do not occur. Indeed, according to Kymlicka, they want to integrate and do not represent a threat to the unity of the state.[42] Their demands for rights should not be interpreted as dangerous signs of separatism, but as the search for 'fair terms of integration'.[43] In other words, those rights that have been identified earlier as polyethnic rights are expressly designed to encourage and enable the integration of immigrants within the dominant culture of the state that receives them, but in accordance with their specific characters. As an example, one can consider the demand for the right of women to wear the veil made by Muslim minorities in Europe.

---

[39] Kymlicka (1995: 108). It should be observed that the fact that cultural minorities may be disadvantaged shows the impossibility of state neutrality in actions relating to cultures. Every public decision differently affects different groups. For example, when a state decides to use a certain language as its official language in public schools, this decision will inevitably favour the majority and disadvantage the minorities. Thus, the idea of benign neglect is, according to Kymlicka, unacceptable. See especially Kymlicka (1995: Chapter VI).

[40] Kymlicka (1995: 113).

[41] Kymlicka (1998: 33).

[42] Kymlicka (1996a: 119).

[43] Kymlicka (2001a: 162).

Liberalism, Minority Rights, and Autonomy

As we have seen, for Kymlicka, the rights of minorities can be accepted by a liberal theory when they do not infringe individual autonomy.[44] The role of autonomy for Kymlicka is so important that he takes it as the foundational value of his liberal theory.[45] Kymlicka understands autonomy as the rational revisability of one's ends. From this perspective, choice is valuable since it allows us to establish and evaluate what is worthy to be pursued. In this sense, the concept of choice and autonomy that Kymlicka adopts is less substantive than the Kantian one (according to which choice has intrinsic value because it reflects the rational nature of human beings), or the Millian one (which instead makes use of the intrinsic value of individuality).[46] Yet, even in this sense, that Kymlicka believes is widely accepted by national minorities and immigrants living in Western liberal democracies, the idea of autonomy is peculiarly problematic.

First, the view that a good life should be an autonomous life (in Kymlicka's meaning) is neither self-evident nor universally shared. In the section on 'Liberalism and Cultural Membership', I identified the conditions that Kymlicka believes are necessary for living a good life—that life should be lived from within and that individuals must be able to review their purposes. These are not propositions that have unanimous acceptance in modern liberal society. As Bhikhu Parekh has written, 'the very idea of living life from the inside is essentially Protestant, and played only a limited role in classical Athens and Rome, medieval Europe, Catholic Christianity and non-western civilizations.'[47] Not even the revisability of one's life plans seems an indisputable prerequisite for the realization of a good life. Think, for instance, of those who build their life around their commitment to a particular end that they take as unquestionable, and then measure their success by the degree or quality of the achievement of that end. In other words, as William Galston has written, 'autonomy is one possible mode of existence in liberal societies—one among many

---

[44] See the first argument in support of the compatibility between minority rights and liberalism.

[45] In a 1996 article, Kymlicka claims that 'the most defensible liberal theory is founded on the value of autonomy'. See Kymlicka (1996b: 95).

[46] Kymlicka (1995: 213).

[47] Parekh (2006: 106).

others.'[48] For this reason, a theory according to which a life is not ethically successful if the subject does not satisfy the two conditions mentioned by Kymlicka seems unable to appreciate and respect the deep diversity that characterizes the modern world.

Even the way in which Kymlicka conceives the value of cultural membership, and of how a moral subject sees her/his relation with her/his own culture, seems disputable and too West oriented.[49] From the perspective of Kymlicka, as mentioned earlier, the individual attaches value to the fact that s/he belongs to a particular culture both because it is the context in which s/he finds the conditions required to live autonomously and because it confers identity on its members. However, for those belonging to traditional minority groups, these two conditions may come into near-unsolvable conflict.

Individuals belonging to traditional groups illustrate the fact that when a culture confers identity on its members, at the same time it limits the likelihood both of individual choice and of members developing as autonomous individuals. In this regard, Monique Deveaux claims that:

> [R]ather than citing 'meaningful individual choice' as the most important benefit of belonging to a culture, members of cultural minority groups could emphasize the ways in which membership gives a sense of belonging—in other words, a safe and stable context that provides emotional and psychological steadiness and helps reduce the chaos and disorientation caused by having too many possible life choices in the modern world.[50]

In cases like these, Kymlicka's emphasis on autonomy might suggest a lack of respect for and understanding of the specificities of certain minorities.

So, in modern liberal democratic societies, there are individuals who belong to some cultural groups, either secular or religious, that attach great value to respect for tradition and conceive the 'good life' within the framework of their cultural membership. A strong emphasis on

[48] Galston (2002a: 24).

[49] Javeed Alam, for instance, has drawn attention to the existence of traditional communities in India for which individual autonomy has no value at all. These communities do not recognize any place for the existence of members understood as individuals. See Alam (1998: 323–47, especially p. 324).

[50] Deveaux (2000: 132).

autonomy could lead to the marginalization of these groups.[51] Margaret Moore has written that 'because culture is valuable in so far as it contributes to the exercise of autonomy, rights to the protection of culture are justified only in the cases of those groups, or those cultures, who attach value to autonomy.'[52] From the perspective of a liberalism based on the value of autonomy, demands for the recognition of rights for minority cultures that do not recognize autonomy's primacy, but could also be in a condition of undeserved disadvantage, would have no legitimacy. This view is, however, in tension with Kymlicka's argument, according to which the attribution of rights to cultural minorities is grounded in the egalitarian premises of liberal theory.

Kymlicka's liberalism explicitly aims at liberalizing non-liberal national minorities,[53] though this process, as Kymlicka points out, should not be coercive. In fact, in *Multicultural Citizenship*, one can find the distinction between the process of identifying the most defensible liberal theory, namely, the one based on autonomy, and the issue of who can exercise the authority to impose this theory on minorities that do not recognize the primacy of liberal values.[54] Except in the case of serious violations of human rights of the individuals involved, for Kymlicka, a direct coercive intervention is not acceptable. What the liberals can do is limited to indirect action and to offering incentives for liberalization. Thus, the ban on the imposition of the principles of liberal theory that, at least in principle, liberals accept in the ambit of the relations between independent nation-states must be considered valid when cultural minorities within a liberal state are concerned.

In a book that in many ways represents a radical alternative to the way in which Kymlicka faces the problem of cultural minorities, Chandran Kukathas has criticized the distinction between the identification of the

---

[51] Mahajan (2014: 61–2).

[52] Moore (2001: 55). One should add that if the recognition of minority rights depends on the promotion of the conditions necessary for the exercise of autonomy, Kymlicka cannot distinguish between 'those clearly illiberal groups who restrict the freedom of their members in coercive ways and those simply non-liberal communities with more heteronomous lifestyles.' The former cannot be tolerated in a liberal democratic order, whereas the last are, under certain conditions, acceptable. See Deveaux (2000: 133).

[53] Kymlicka (1995: 95).

[54] Kymlicka (1995: 163–70).

most adequate liberal theory and the imposition of the theory itself on those who do not share its tenets. With the refusal to impose liberalism, Kymlicka would grant to minorities many of those internal restrictions that, as the previous sections have shown, are not acceptable within his approach. According to Kukathas, therefore, Kymlicka's theory is inconsistent: '[H]e proposes to embrace "comprehensive" liberalism, and its commitment to autonomy, but *not* to enforce this liberalism.'[55] I do not think, however, that the refusal to impose a pro-autonomy liberal theory shows that Kymlicka's theory is inconsistent. The anti-imposition stance is, rather, a way to avoid the defeat of one of the premises for the realization of a good life for the people belonging to minority groups. In fact, as shown in the section 'Liberalism and Cultural Membership', among the rules for leading a good life is that life should be led from the inside, namely, according to values endorsed by the individual. If an independent lifestyle was to be coercively imposed, those who would suffer the imposition would be forced to live according to values of which they do not approve.

Even if the presence of these considerations shows Kymlicka's caution in imposing liberalism, I contend that his approach, because of its attempt to liberalize minorities, is nonetheless unable to respect minorities in their specificities. The liberalization of minorities, as Parekh has rightly observed, could 'transform them into something they are not'.[56] There is nothing to object to in the fact that culture transforms. In fact, unless one shares the implausible view that cultures are unchanging, isolated entities, we must admit that historical circumstances and reciprocal relationships are tirelessly at work to promote their change and development. The problems for a theory that intends to keep faith with the principles of egalitarian liberalism arise when one considers that it is always the minority culture that transforms, and that this transformation takes place according to criteria endorsed by the majority culture. So, the balance of power between cultural groups is not challenged. This view is in clear tension both with one of the principles that Kymlicka deemed to be related to the spread of liberal multiculturalism, namely, the idea that the state does not belong to the cultural majority group but is the property of all its citizens regardless of their community, and with the egalitarianism that generally characterizes the liberal approach of Kymlicka.

[55] Kukathas (2003: 108).
[56] Parekh (2006: 108).

In partial response to such an objection, in *Multicultural Odysseys*, Kymlicka claims that 'the liberal view of multiculturalism is inevitably, intentionally, and unapologetically transformational of people's cultural traditions.'[57] It requires that both the dominant and the subject groups enter into relationships and are involved in practices requiring changes to both parties. In this sense, the majority group is required to 'renounce fantasies of racial superiority, to relinquish claims to exclusive owner-ship of the state, and to abandon attempts to fashion public institutions solely in its own national (typically white/Christian) image'.[58] In other words, majorities are asked to be faithful to liberal democratic principles. Considering, though, that the majorities we are dealing with are mainly liberal democratic, the demands are not very burdensome for them. Minorities, on their part, are required to reject practices that are incom-patible with liberal democratic principles—such as racial prejudice, anti-Semitism, political authoritarianism, and so on—even if these practices are vital to their existence and perpetuation.

It is impossible to deny that Kymlicka's view on the integration of minorities[59] represents a significant step forward compared to a purely assimilationist approach, according to which minorities have to change to the point of becoming indistinguishable from the majority. Nonetheless, a sort of asymmetry in favour of the strongest group still remains. The majority is required to transform itself in accordance with its own principles, although these same very principles sometimes are not respected for historical accidents or negligence. Minorities, for their part, are asked to conform to standards which, to varying degrees, are not theirs.

The Diversity of Immigrants between Assimilation and Integration

As seen in the section, 'Cultural Pluralism and Minority Rights', Kymlicka identifies immigration as the second source of cultural diversity.

---

[57] Kymlicka (2007c: 99).

[58] Kymlicka (2007c: 99–100).

[59] Note that these thoughts are, among other things, in line with the view that the integration of immigrants is a two-way street, about which I will talk more extensively in the next section.

Immigration is seen as a largely voluntary phenomenon[60] and migrants are considered to be generally available to integrate into the society that receives them. They do not seek, nor do they have the ability to recreate, the social culture of the country of origin but, by requiring specific policy measures, they search an integration that is as fair as possible. So, both immigrants and the liberal policies of the state concerning them do not have the goal of segregation or self-segregation, except in cases of some conservative minorities like the Amish.

In *Politics in the Vernacular*, Kymlicka approvingly argues that since the 1960s, in the three countries that face the problem of immigration the most (USA, Canada, and Australia), there has been a shift from the so-called model of 'Anglo-conformity'[61] to a less assimilationist and more tolerant political attitude. According to the Anglo-conformity model, immigrants must adopt in every respect the cultural practices and identity of the country they move to, until they become culturally indistinguishable from the natives. The policies adopted since the 1960s tend to see the integration of immigrants as consistent with the preservation of their cultural specificity. Kymlicka assumes that immigrants want to participate in the life of the country in which they have settled, as citizens worthy of equal consideration and respect. They not only have the right but also the duty[62] to become full members of their new political community. Far from being a process that requires sacrifice exclusively by immigrants, integration is a 'two-way street'[63] because the presence of immigrants also changes the receiving society. In particular, the immigration policy of a liberal state aims at achieving what has been defined as 'pluralistic

[60] To the idea that immigration is a voluntary phenomenon, there have often been objections. See, for instance, Kukathas (1997a: 412–16). The voluntariness of immigration has been critically discussed also by Tariq Modood. He points out the difficulty of considering voluntary the big immigration movements after the Second World War: They should be understood as movements connected to the dissolution of the colonies. See Modood (2013: 31).

[61] Kymlicka (2001a: 153).

[62] In an essay about the extension of the domain of justice in a liberal egalitarian perspective, Kymlicka (2001b: 263) argues that 'liberal democracies not only allow the integration of immigrants, but exert pressures so that happens. Immigrants have not only the right to become fully members of the nation, but even the duty to become part of the national community'.

[63] Kymlicka (2001a: 171).

integration'.[64] The majority societal culture, following the entry of ethnic minorities that are carriers of specific cultural identities, becomes more diverse. At the same time, in contact with those of the receiving society, the habits and practices of immigrants change as well.

Kymlicka's theory runs into trouble once again because of its reliance on the value of autonomy. It seems to me that his generous attempt to discuss the reciprocity of the transformations involved in the process of inclusion of immigrants can be objected to for reasons analogous to the ones considered in the preceding section of this chapter, when the liberalization of national minorities was in focus. In what follows, I will discuss the failure of Kymlicka's theory to deal with the cultural diversity represented by immigrants.

The difficulties faced by Kymlicka's theory in coping with the problem of ethnic minorities can be explained with what Tariq Modood has called 'multinational bias'.[65] Notwithstanding its pragmatic generosity (think of the aforementioned idea of 'pluralistic integration'), Kymlicka's approach is 'theoretically ungenerous'[66] towards the members of ethnic minorities. In fact, the provision of rights in favour of minority cultures is based on individual membership in a societal culture. Immigrants, according to Kymlicka's model, neither possess nor plan to create a societal culture in the society in which they move. Thus, for immigrants, there is no specific argument that warrants some rights with the same bindingness of national minorities' rights. One reason for the multinational bias is, according to Modood, Kymlicka's Canadian origins and his enduring interest in national minorities in Canada and USA. From that descends, again according to Modood, the poor applicability of Kymlicka's model to the analysis of the matter of cultural diversity in all those contexts in which immigration represents a much more sensible and urgent problem than national minorities.[67]

I think that the limits of Kymlicka's approach in dealing with ethnic minorities should mainly be attributed to the fact that the cultural diversity represented by immigrants is widely undervalued in comparison

---

[64] Kymlicka (2001a: 168). This expression can be also found in Spinner-Halev (1994: Chapter IV).

[65] Modood (2013: 32).

[66] Modood (2013: 32).

[67] Modood (2013).

with national minorities' diversity. For example, in an article in which he responds to concerns about a general decline of multicultural policies in Western liberal democracies, Kymlicka contends that 'the claims of national groups and indigenous peoples generally imply a more substantial input of diversity in the public sphere and a much more substantial level of differentiated citizenship than what is required by immigrants' groups.'[68] However, if we consider that national minorities and indigenous peoples are concentrated in a different territory from the one in which the majority resides, and given that they are culturally independent (according to Kymlicka himself), it is difficult to understand how the diversity they represent is present in the public sphere of a liberal country, except in a very indirect and attenuated form. Immigrants, by contrast, are not territorially concentrated in an area and mostly tend not to take an isolationist attitude. So, the diversity they introduce in the society in which they move is much more perceivable. Immigrants' practices and values coexist, sometimes peacefully and sometimes in conflict, with majority practices and values. It is this kind of diversity that a liberal society should take as having priority, and it is to the need to accommodate it fairly that the classical liberal principles of equality, freedom, and inclusion should be applied.

At the moment, as a matter of fact, the pluralist integration advocated by Kymlicka has not yet been achieved. Rather, in recent years, we have witnessed the spread of a climate of distrust towards multicultural policies, especially those aimed at immigrants.[69] It is likely, and desirable too, that all the discussion on the death of multiculturalism is more an exaggeration than the expression of a concrete reality.[70] The fact remains that,

---

[68] Kymlicka (2007b: 51).

[69] Kymlicka thinks that the three main reasons for the decrease of support for multicultural policies among the public are: the increasing number of illegal immigrants; the idea that immigrants (especially in case of Muslim immigrants) are bearers of illiberal cultures; and the perception that the presence of immigrants weakens the welfare state. These are, for Kymlicka, only contingent factors and once they are settled, the acceptance of multiculturalism can be restored. In other words, in 'countries where immigrants are seen as legally admitted, as complying with liberal norms, and as net economic contributors, then adopting multiculturalism is seen as low risk and will face the fewest obstacles.' See Kymlicka (2007b: 56).

[70] Kymlicka (2012: 14).

regardless of the alleged failure of multicultural policies, liberal multiculturalism has some fundamental weaknesses at the theoretical level. Thus, if the thoughts presented in these pages have some plausibility, a model such as Kymlicka's, based on the idea that autonomy is the fundamental value of liberalism and on the view that in the discourse on the rights of minorities the diversity of national minorities must have priority, is doomed to fail.

Liberal Pluralism and Diversity

This chapter will discuss comprehensive pro-toleration liberalism (CT liberalism). William Galston's views will be studied as an illustration of how CT liberalism faces the problem of diversity. His work on liberalism is a noteworthy attempt to deal with the subject discussed in this book.[1] Indeed, his concept of *diversity liberalism* is one of the most stimulating, though deeply questionable, answers to the problem of accommodating diversity. Insofar as it eschews any commitment to the primacy of autonomy, Galston's theory represents a significant improvement in comparison with Will Kymlicka's approach, at least in terms of practical accommodation of diversity. However, as I will argue in this chapter, Galston's reliance on value pluralism, together with other aspects of his theory, make CT liberalism strongly objectionable.

The next section will present Galston's theoretical proposal as an approach alternative to *autonomy liberalism*. Then, there will be an analysis of expressive liberty, political pluralism, and value pluralism, which are the three theoretical pillars on which diversity liberalism relies. In the following section, the focus will be on educational policy, considered to be a domain in which the tenets of Galston's approach are particularly relevant. In the concluding section, some critical remarks will illustrate the overall inadequacy of Galston's diversity liberalism.

---

[1] See especially Galston (2002a, 2005).

Liberalism between Autonomy and Diversity

In an article, Galston has defined liberalism as a theory concerned with limits to public power: 'From a philosophical and conceptual point of view, liberalism is a doctrine not of the structure of governmental decision making or of the substance of governmental decisions, but rather of the scope of governmental power.'[2] Every liberal theory is characterized by an account of the ways in which the extension of public power should be limited, and it is just this view on the limits of the power that entitles a theory to be considered liberal. For example, John Stuart Mill can be included among liberal thinkers not because of his ideas on 'human flourishing', but thanks to his 'harm principle'. Similarly, John Rawls is a liberal for his account of individual rights, not for his theory of distributive justice and his 'difference principle'.[3]

For Galston, liberalism is not a monolithic political and theoretical tradition. There are at least two concepts of liberalism, that is, 'two quite different strands of liberal thought based on two distinct principles'[4], that can be summarized as autonomy and diversity.[5]

Autonomy liberalism has its roots in Enlightenment liberalism. Galston argues that the historical and conceptual origins of this kind of liberal theory are to be found in the Enlightenment's faith in reason as the primary source of authority and as the necessary means for liberating individuals from arbitrary power. According to this theory, the state should promote and defend individual autonomy, understood as the ability of individuals to govern their lives without the imposition of norms, values, and preferences from any external source. Autonomy can be promoted through educational policies based on autonomous, individualistic, and rationalistic theories of human flourishing. The defence and propagation of autonomy, as understood in Enlightenment liberalism, is to be pursued by means of anti-accommodationist policies aimed at those groups that do not value autonomy as a fundamental condition for human thriving.

---

[2] Galston (2007b: 290).

[3] Galston (2007b: 290)

[4] Galston (1995: 521).

[5] This distinction, as explained in the first chapter, can be used to interpret all of liberal history. See Levy (2003).

According to Galston, Locke, Kant, Mill, and some American scholars influenced by Emerson are the most representative advocates of autonomy liberalism.[6] Among the contemporary autonomy liberals, we find Kymlicka, who, as shown in Chapter 2 of this book, establishes a link between the promotion of individual autonomy and the protection of minority cultures, which is considered as the milieu that individuals need for making meaningful choices.[7] Other examples include Rawls, who, in *A Theory of Justice*,[8] overtly relies upon a Kantian notion of the moral subject, and Stephen Macedo, who, in *Liberal Virtues*,[9] works out a theory of liberal citizenship in which autonomy is highly emphasized as the distinctive feature of the character of a liberal person.

Galston thinks that autonomy liberalism may be the subject of a crucial critique. As mentioned in the previous chapter, he objects to it on the grounds that being autonomous is just one way, not the only way, of living in a free society.[10] If public institutions assume the primacy of autonomy, individuals and groups who deny that autonomy is always required for human thriving could feel jeopardized by and alienated from a political power that does not adequately respect human diversity. These considerations lie behind the widespread notion that liberalism is no more than a sectarian doctrine, in spite of its declared aspirations to impartiality, neutrality, and universality. Galston maintains that 'autonomy based arguments are bound to marginalize those individuals and groups who cannot conscientiously embrace the Enlightenment impulse.'[11] In fact, our societies are populated by many individuals and groups whose ideals of human flourishing are in no way associated with autonomous choice, critical self-reflection, and all those attitudes generally linked with a liberal–rationalistic idea of the individual.

[6] Galston (2002a: 21).

[7] See Kymlicka (1989a, 1995).

[8] Rawls (1999a).

[9] Macedo (1990: 269). In 'Two Concepts of Liberalism', Galston (1995: 523) quotes the following passage from a book by Stephen Macedo as a typical example of autonomy liberalism: 'Liberal persons are distinguished by the possession of self-governing reflective capacities. Further developing these reflective capacities leads one toward the ideal of autonomy.'

[10] Galston (2002a: 24).

[11] Galston (2002a: 25–6).

Galston has been criticizing autonomy liberalism for a long time. In his 1991 book, *Liberal Purposes*, he has argued against those theorists according to whom civic education should be aimed at the promotion of those rational attitudes needed for critically evaluating and choosing among different moral options. In the book, he has written that, properly understood, 'liberalism is about the protection of diversity, not the valorization of choice.'[12] Indeed, the liberal model that Galston prefers is diversity liberalism. He calls it also Reformation liberalism, because he thinks its roots can be traced back to the post-Reformation idea of toleration. It is the liberalism that 'takes as its central value the toleration of religious and cultural diversity'.[13] Such liberalism conceives of diversity as 'legitimate differences among individuals and groups over such matters as the nature of good life, sources of moral authority, reason versus faith, and the like'.[14]

Taking the protection of diversity as the core value of the political theory allows diversity liberalism to pursue what Galston labels 'a policy of *maximum feasible accommodation*'.[15] This is a policy that assigns maximum possible space to diversity, provided that civic unity and individual security are not jeopardized. Moreover, diversity liberalism enables political institutions to take diversity seriously, without imposing liberal values on the internal life of those groups that live in contemporary liberal societies but are not willing to accept the idea that autonomy and individual choice, understood along liberal lines, are the conditions humans need in order to flourish.

It should be clear from the foregoing that Galston's acceptance of diversity is not without limits. In fact, the constraints imposed on the diversity that a liberal state can accept are quite demanding. Far from committing to the idea of liberal neutrality,[16] Galston sees the liberal state as a political community that pursues public purposes, such as the protection of human life, the advancement of basic human capabilities, the development of the abilities necessary for taking part in public life, and

---

[12] Galston (1991: 329). The main target of his critical remarks is Gutmann (1999).

[13] Crowder (2007: 123).

[14] Galston (2002a: 21).

[15] Galston (2002a: 20).

[16] For his objection to liberal neutrality, see Galston (1991: Part 2).

so on. These public purposes make the unity of a liberal society possible, give shape to its institutions, guide public policy, and establish what is virtuous from the public point of view. Thus, a community that, in practice, denies any of these public purposes would be beyond the domain of admissible diversity in a liberal state.

I would like to point out here that Galston's preference for diversity liberalism is not so strong as 'to deny a place for a more modest conception of autonomy as freedom of choice, secured by internal as well as external constraints'.[17] Galston's declared intention, consistent with his pluralist account of value (discussed later in this chapter), is to balance the two dimensions of liberalism that he distinguishes. Notwithstanding this, as our further considerations will demonstrate and one commentator argues, 'Galston's emphasis has always been on the toleration side'[18] rather than on autonomy.

Sources of Liberal Theory and Galston's Liberal Pluralism

As stated earlier, Galston's diversity liberalism relies on three pillars: expressive liberty, political pluralism, and value pluralism. Expressive liberty is 'the normatively privileged and institutionally defended ability of individuals and groups to lead their lives as they see fit'.[19] Individuals want to live a life in which there is correspondence between inner beliefs and outer practices[20]—that is to say, they want to live according to their

---

[17] Galston (2005: 182).

[18] Crowder (2007: 124).

[19] Galston (2005: 45). From this quote, it is clear that expressive liberty concerns individuals as well as groups. In another passage, Galston (2002a: 28) defines expressive liberty as 'the absence of constraints, imposed by some individuals on others, that make it impossible (or significantly more difficult) for the affected individuals to live their lives in ways that express their deepest beliefs about what gives meaning or value to life'. It would seem that, in this definition, expressive liberty is more a property of individuals than of groups, but on the following page Galston's usual emphasis on groups reappears: 'Expressive liberty protects the ability of individuals and groups to live in ways that others would regard as unfree' (Galston 2002a: 29).

[20] If expressive liberty, as Galston thinks, is an individual as well as a group liberty, here one should say that a group also wants that its collective life should be consistent with the principles it values. From a liberal and individualist point of

conceptions of what is valuable and meaningful. They think that there is loss of a fundamental human good when they are coercively deprived of the opportunity to lead their life in a way that is consistent with their considered judgement. Obviously, Galston admits that expressive liberty has limits and that not every practice is to be accommodated just because it arises from a sincere belief. For example, respect for expressive liberty does not lead a society to the acceptance of human sacrifice for religious or conscientious reasons. On the contrary, some practices of conservative groups (such as male circumcision or gender separation) that would be condemned by autonomy liberals might be consistent with expressive liberty.

Political pluralism is the second pillar upon which Galston's liberalism rests. It is the political theory worked out by John Neville Figgis, George Douglas Howard Cole, and Harold Laski[21] in the first decades of the twentieth century. Political pluralism does not accept the idea that state power is omnipotent regarding the plurality of associations and groups in contemporary liberal democratic societies. According to political pluralists, power should not be in the hands of a single elite but should be dispersed among a plurality of groups. Galston argues that political pluralism is an effective tool for alerting us to the risks deriving from the totalistic temptations traceable in the thoughts of Aristotle, Hobbes, and Rousseau. Aristotle maintained that all institutions and social life should be subordinated to politics, as it is politics that aims at the highest and most comprehensive human good. Hobbes argued in favour of an undivided sovereignty as the only guarantee of peace. Finally, Rousseau considered an unreserved commitment to the common good a necessary condition for civic health. The same totalistic temptation is still present in the ideas of many contemporary theorists working within the liberal framework. For example, according to Galston, Macedo's *transformative liberalism* ends up requiring the correspondence between public political

---

view, arguing that groups have a collective life and follow some set of principles is always problematic. What are these principles? Are they to rule only political life or should their domain include private life? How should such principles be identified? Galston never clearly addresses these questions, and, as we will see later, his commitment both to individual and to group expressive liberty can create tensions that raise doubt about the overall liberal character of his theory.

[21] See Hirst (1989).

principles and the internal structure of associations, faith communities, and even families.[22]

Political pluralists' core idea is that 'our social life comprises multiple sources of authority and sovereignty—individuals, parents, associations, churches, and state institutions, among others—no one of which is dominant for all purposes and on all occasions.'[23] In a liberal setting, there are several non-state authorities whose existence is independent of state power. Thus, a centralized state authority is not the only lawful authority exercising power. In *The Practice of Liberal Pluralism*, Galston writes that 'pluralist politics is a politics of recognition rather than of construction.'[24] Different spheres of human activity exist and are to be recognized and respected by the state, although they are not created by it. For example, even if one admits that public rules shape families' internal lives, this does not mean that families themselves are purposively constituted by the state.

From the perspective of political pluralism, the function of the state is constrained but not nullified. In this sense, Galston asserts that the state, which is the only authority with a monopoly over the legitimate use of force, should coordinate the activities of different communities, adjudicate conflicts, and prevent group tyrannies. The risk of group tyrannies is especially relevant for any liberal theory that accords value to the right of association. On his part, Galston deals quite optimistically with such a threat, claiming that 'enforcement of basic rights of citizenship and of exit rights, suitably understood',[25] will be a strong enough guarantee to prevent any group becoming a prison for individuals who are born into and educated within it, or even for those who join such a group as adults.

---

[22] See Galston's (2002b). Galston refers to Macedo's ideas about the pervasiveness of political principles in a well-functioning liberal democracy. Liberal principles extensively shape the life of communities, associations, and even churches, transforming them in the liberal sense. Other contemporary examples of liberal democratic theorists giving up to the totalistic temptation, according to Galston, are Jurgen Habermas, John Dewey, John Rawls, Amy Gutmann, Ian Shapiro, and Dennis Thompson. See Galston (2005: 26–40).

[23] Galston (2002a: 36).

[24] Galston (2005: 41).

[25] Galston (2005: 41).

The third resource of Galston's liberalism is value pluralism. It is a form of moral realism[26] deriving from Isaiah Berlin[27] and distinct from emotivism, non-cognitivism, or 'Humean arguments against the rational status of moral propositions'.[28] Galston has summarized value pluralism in the following five propositions:[29]

1. 'Value pluralism is not relativism.'[30] It allows the distinction between what is good and what is bad, and recognizes the objectivity of moral values. Value pluralists, in fact, can claim that saving a human life is different from killing innocent people and that this difference is 'part of the objective structure of the valuational universe'.[31]

2. Value pluralists argue that 'objective goods cannot be fully rank-ordered'.[32] Goods are heterogeneous and, in moral life, there is no unique *summum bonum* that everyone recognizes as the chief value. This means that we cannot have lexical orderings of moral goods and that the importance of virtues and goods depends on circumstances.

3. 'Some goods are basic in the sense that they form part of any choice-worthy conception of human life.'[33] There is a domain of values that establishes what constitutes a decent life for individuals and societies.[34] Galston, following Stuart Hampshire, argues that the

---

[26] For Galston (2005: 12), value pluralism is a form of moral realism because it 'presupposes the existence of a moral realm that is in some sense "there", apart from our emotional projections and cultural constructions'.

[27] For Berlin's political thought and the ways in which his value pluralism is linked to liberalism, see Crowder (2004) and Crowder and Hardy (2007).

[28] Galston (2002a: 30).

[29] Galston (2009: 804–5).

[30] Galston (2002a: 5).

[31] Galston (2002a: 30). On the differences between pluralism and relativism, see Parekh (2011: 74–5).

[32] Galston (2002a: 5).

[33] Galston (2002a: 6).

[34] Here, Galston is explicitly influenced by H.L.A. Hart on the minimum content of natural law (see Hart [1961:189–95]). As he stated in an interview, 'there are certain goods that no human being would willingly do without, and political authority behaves wrongly when it disregards or contradicts this fact, which is ... at the heart of international human rights standards.' See Galston (2006: 120). He does not want to introduce natural law elements in his theory. Rather, his aim is to point out that there are *great evils* of the human condition with which politics should be concerned.

limits are fixed 'by common human needs'[35] and in many historical circumstances, these limits have been overcome.

4. 'Beyond this parsimonious list of basic goods, there is a wide range of legitimate diversity' within which individual liberty can be practised.[36]

5. 'Value pluralism is distinguished from various forms of what I will call "monism".'[37] The latter claims that all moral values can be reduced to a single measure and that all moral questions have, at least in principle, a clear and identifiable solution. Utilitarianism is a classical and well-known expression of monist theory. Whereas Rawls and other deontological theorists have objected to utilitarianism on the grounds that it does not adequately respect the separateness of persons,[38] value pluralists' objection concerns the fact that 'utilitarianism fails to take seriously the heterogeneity of values.'[39] According to Galston, it is utilitarianism (and all other variants of monist theories) that should demonstrate how the heterogeneity of goods is reducible to homogeneity without improperly reducing the complexity of our ordinary moral world.

What is distinctive about value pluralism is the incommensurability of values. As Alex Zakaras writes, 'values cannot be arranged neatly into a hierarchy of importance, so that every conflict between values could be arbitrated through appeal to some higher value.'[40] Value pluralism rules out the possibility of fully rank-ordering the distinct and conflicting values that people encounter in their moral and political life. From the point of view of value pluralism, there is also no one value or good that always has priority in case of conflict with other values and goods.

I would like to point out here that Galston never justifies value pluralism. He presents it as 'an account of the actual structure of the normative universe',[41] advances descriptive claims in its favour, and declares that 'it is concrete experience that provides the most compelling reasons

[35] Hampshire (1983: 155).
[36] Galston (2002a: 6).
[37] Galston (2002a: 6).
[38] Rawls (1999a: 164).
[39] Galston (2002a: 33).
[40] Zakaras (2013: 72).
[41] Galston (2002a: 30).

for accepting some form of value pluralism.'[42] What Galston gives us is no more than a description and a defence[43] of value pluralism in response to some objections raised by critics, never a proper philosophical justification.

The political implications of value pluralism are not immediately clear. The compatibility between value pluralism and liberalism is a matter of dispute even among those theorists who accept this account of the moral world. Philosophers like Isaiah Berlin, Bernard Williams, and George Crowder claim that pluralism goes with liberalism.[44] In contrast, others like John Gray believe that the acceptance of value pluralism and the consequent rebuttal of autonomy as the trump value lead to liberalism seen as a theory of only local authority.[45] Still other theorists have remarked upon the indeterminacy of value pluralism as far as politics is concerned. For instance, Robert Talisse has stressed that 'value pluralism has no determinate political prescriptions.'[46]

This chapter, rather than giving a full account of the relation between value pluralism and liberalism, will expound (and afterwards evaluate) Galston's version of this relation. It should be pointed out that in Galston's theory, there is no relation of logical entailment between value pluralism and liberalism.[47] As noted at the beginning of this section, value pluralism is only one of the three independent 'pillars' of diversity liberalism. This means, among other things, that political pluralism and expressive liberty (the other two pillars) are not mere inferences derived from value pluralism. On the contrary, together with value pluralism, they are constitutive components of diversity liberalism.

Galston explicitly follows Berlin's route in trying to elaborate a liberal theory that assumes value pluralism and negative liberty as fundamental

---

[42] Galston (2002a: 33).

[43] See Galston (2005: Chapter 2).

[44] See Berlin (1969), Williams (1978), and Crowder (2002), respectively.

[45] Gray (1996, 2000a). Another position is represented by John Kekes (1996), according to whom value pluralism leads to a rejection of liberalism in politics. For a well-informed survey of the different positions, see Crowder, 'Value Pluralism and Liberalism: Berlin and Beyond', in Crowder and Hardy (2007).

[46] Talisse (2011: 84). In a similar vein, Zakaras (2013: 70) has argued that 'value pluralism yields only indeterminate political conclusions.'

[47] Galston (2013: 98).

ideas. For Galston and Berlin, negative liberty should be considered as 'the capacity of individuals, unimpeded by external coercion or constraint, to choose for themselves among competing conceptions of good or valuable lives'.[48] A minimal conception of liberty such as this can have a privileged status in value pluralism and can function as the starting point for the elaboration of a form of liberalism compatible with value pluralism.

Accepting this idea of negative liberty does not involve committing to controversial metaphysical, philosophical, or psychological systems. What matters is only 'the absence of force'[49] when a member wishes to leave a community that risks becoming as oppressive as a prison. Galston claims that 'this rejection of human imprisonment is the core of what Berlin means by negative liberty',[50] and it is a principle whose moral force is supposed to be acknowledged across political boundaries. Pluralism can accept traditional practices such as arranged marriage, but it cannot accept that a community impose these practices on individuals who refuse to participate in them and who would prefer to leave the community. That is the main meaning of the negative liberty that Galston strives to defend.

It is quite commonly agreed that value pluralism is difficult to reconcile with theories according to which autonomous life is the necessary condition for human flourishing. In this regard, value pluralists stress that there are many goods other than autonomy itself and that a person can lead a good life without being autonomous. However, Galston maintains that this objection does not represent a threat to the centrality of negative liberty in his (and Berlin's) account of value pluralism. Rather, it is 'the fact of value pluralism itself that gives special status to individual liberty'.[51] It is value pluralism's emphasis on the plurality of valuable and ultimate ends that confers particular importance on negative liberty and on the freedom to choose among many options. Galston, consistent with the acceptance of value pluralism, concedes that there are good human lives lived by some who do not ascribe to 'choice' any priority in comparison with other values. At the same time, he recognizes that value pluralism itself suggests that 'there is a range of indeterminacy within

---

[48] Galston (2002a: 48). See also Berlin (1969: Chapter 3).
[49] Galston (2002a: 51).
[50] Galston (2002a: 56).
[51] Galston (2002a: 51).

which various choices are rationally defensible' and that '[b]ecause there is no single uniquely rational ordering or combination of such values',[52] any imposition of an ordering of value would be unjustified.

Thus, the centrality of negative liberty in Galston's (and Berlin's) value pluralism is rooted not in the belief that rational and conscious choice is a feature that necessarily distinguishes the good lives, but in the idea that coercion, not being a natural fact, should be always justified[53] because of the 'pervasive human desire to go our own way in accordance with our own desires and beliefs'.[54] This desire should not be interpreted as an equivalent of the idea of liberal autonomy and as an endorsement of the view that autonomy is always the trumping value. In fact, this move would be unavailable to value pluralists given their commitment to the view that there is no such value. Galston insists that the desire to live in accordance with one's own conception of life is not a desire for an autonomous life. 'A life lived with the requisite symmetry between the inner and the outer is a life of integrity',[55] he writes, and when this symmetry occurs unimpeded by external force, even non-autonomous lives can achieve a significant level of integrity.

To give a more complete presentation of Galston's liberal pluralism, I conclude this section with some remarks about the *comprehensive* character of Galston's theory in comparison with Rawlsian *political* liberalism. The comprehensiveness of liberal pluralism descends in quite obvious ways from its reliance on value pluralism. According to Galston, this is one of the crucial aspects of his approach, insofar as it makes it possible 'to connect what one believes to be the best account of public life with

---

[52] Galston (2002a: 57).

[53] Galston's argument on negative liberty has been criticized by Talisse (2004: 133) since it appears to rely, without sufficient reason, on the idea that negative liberty plays the role of the 'default position'; for similar comments, see Ceva (2005). This role is so crucial that any deviation from negative liberty needs to be justified. In addition, according to Talisse, any illiberal group seems to be under a burden of proof. Galston has attempted to reply to this critique by pointing out that his account of negative liberty is not be read as the identification of an arbitrary default position, but should be related to the classical problem of the justification of political authority and to the fact that value pluralism cannot be impartial among all the justificatory strategies. See Galston (2004: 146).

[54] Galston (2002a: 58).

[55] Galston (2005: 192).

comparably persuasive accounts of morality, human psychology, and the natural world'.[56] However, given what has been said in the first chapter, this connection between public life and other kinds of commitments contradicts political liberalism's tenets. In fact, as Charles Larmore has written, political liberalism's ambition is to 'find principles of political association expressing certain fundamental moral values that, to as great an extent as possible, reasonable people[57] may accept despite the different views about the good and about religious truth that divide them'.[58] Value pluralism, as the previous pages show, is a complex view about the nature of value in plain opposition to those metaphysical and religious doctrines according to which there is only a single source of value. From the standpoint of political liberalism, it appears to be such a controversial doctrine that its claims can reasonably be rejected.

Galston's divergence from political liberalism can be seen also in the different ways in which each accounts for the scope of political theory and justification. Rawls thinks about a liberal theory whose scope is limited to the basic structure of society, is independent (or 'freestanding') from comprehensive doctrines, and is worked out from values, ideas, and principles implicit in the culture of a liberal democratic society.[59] Rawlsian political liberalism demands that the public justification of fundamental institutions and policies must rely on public reasons and avoid any appeal to contested and controversial comprehensive doctrines.[60] Galston's liberal pluralism has deeper ambitions. In fact, Galston claims that it is impossible to submit political discourse to the extremely demanding constraints of Rawlsian public reason.[61] Public discussion of policies

[56] Galston (2007a: 252).

[57] Note that here 'people' is synonymous of 'persons'. Reasonable persons here should be seen in Rawlsian terms, namely, as those persons who want 'a social world in which they, as free and equal, can cooperate with others on terms all can accept. They insist that reciprocity should hold within that world so that each benefits along with others.' See Rawls (2005: 50).

[58] Larmore (1996: 154).

[59] See Chapter 1.

[60] See Chapter 4 for an account of public justification and public reason in political liberalism. Comprehensive doctrines have been defined in Chapter 1.

[61] To tell the truth, Galston's is a too-rigid and schematic rendering of Rawlsian political liberalism and of his idea of public reason, which, in more recent reformulations, admits some substantial detours from the strictness criticized by

and constitutional matters cannot avoid reference to contested notions deriving from comprehensive doctrines. Abortion is a typical example of a morally and politically controversial issue in which every collective decision implies reference to some disputed doctrine. Both 'pro-life' and 'pro-choice' decisions exhibit a commitment to specific ideas of personality, of the meaning of human life, and of right moral behaviour.[62] The alternative 'is stubborn silence, a kind of democratic dogmatism that ill serves both theory and practice'.[63]

Educating for Diversity

A concise discussion about educational policies will illustrate how Galston's diversity liberalism actually deals with practical cases. Indeed, education is a field that can be particularly troublesome in cases concerning the accommodation of the demands of individuals and groups who do not perceive their flourishing in autonomy terms. For instance, consider traditional communities within a liberal democracy that, for religious reasons, refuse to assimilate and instead try to shield themselves from scientific progress, ideals of civic participation, self-criticism, individuality, and other values that mark modernity. Such communities represent a thorny challenge to liberalism's aspirations to inclusiveness and fairness.

The Amish are the classic and most-debated example of such groups, because they are involved in *Wisconsin* v. *Yoder*, one of the best-known US judicial cases concerning education.[64] The Amish constitute small and conservative religious communities living in North America, mainly in Pennsylvania and the Midwest, USA, and Ontario, Canada. They completely reject the lifestyles of the modern world and attempt to live according to their religious norms. These norms command isolation from the secular world, the rejection of technology, and a severe system

---

Galston. In fact, in Rawls's later works, appeals to comprehensive doctrines are considered acceptable in certain circumstances. See Rawls (1997).

[62] Galston (1982: 627).

[63] Galston (2002a: 44).

[64] *Wisconsin* v. *Yoder*, 406 US 205 (1972). For a more detailed account of the Amish communities and *Wisconsin* v. *Yoder*, see Arneson and Shapiro (1996), Gutmann (1980) and Spinner-Halev (1994: Chapter 5).

of education designed to prepare young Amish to perpetuate their community without questioning its structure or criticizing its practices. As Arneson and Shapiro observe, the Amish are 'particularly opposed to high school education, which they see as threatening to their entire way of life'.[65]

In *Wisconsin v. Yoder*, three Amish parents requested and obtained for their children exemption from two years of high school—years which were mandated under a Wisconsin state law that prescribed school attendance till the age of 16. The Amish parents claimed that, for their children, going to public schools in the same classrooms with other non-Amish pupils would have represented an excess of exposure to diversity of lifestyles, world views, and religious beliefs. Such contact with different people and cultures, the Amish parents alleged, would have been prejudicial to the preservation of the integrity of their way of life. They also claimed that, particularly in the last two years of compulsory education, Amish children would have been likely to develop critical attitudes that would have encouraged them to leave the community. Moreover, the Amish parents maintained that making high-school education compulsory would have been both contrary to their religious beliefs and an unjust curtailment of their religious freedom.

Galston claims that 'Yoder was correctly decided.'[66] Taking this stance, Galston differentiates himself both from those conservatives who fear that admitting exemptions from general laws for religious groups could weaken state power and from those liberals who argue that exemptions like those allowed by Yoder could translate into obstacles to the development of autonomy in children. I argue that the best way to make sense of Galston's endorsement of Yoder has to make reference to expressive liberty, political pluralism, and value pluralism, namely, the three sources of his liberal pluralism. Thus, in the rest of this section, I will demonstrate how each of the three pillars accounts for Galston's approval of Yoder.

The expressive liberty at stake in the discussion on children's education is parents' expressive liberty.[67] Galston argues that 'the ability of

---

[65] Arneson and Shapiro (1996: 141).

[66] Galston (1995: 516).

[67] This is the only expressive liberty explicitly acknowledged by Galston in the case I am considering here, but, as remarked in Note 19 in this chapter, Galston admits that even groups are the kinds of subjects to which expressive liberty

parents to raise their children in a manner consistent with their deepest commitments is an essential element of expressive liberty.'[68] He partially accepts the *fiduciary model*,[69] according to which parents should promote the future interests of their children. The main reasons in favour of this model are children's 'vulnerability, dependency, and developmental needs'.[70]

Galston argues that, in raising children, parents are not mere caretakers. They are not even teachers or state agents whose main role is to create good citizens. Relying on some of Eamonn Callan's reflections on the child–parent relationship, Galston writes that 'parenting is typically undertaken as one of the central meaning-giving tasks of our lives.'[71] In fact, being a good parent is a fundamental part of what constitutes a good life for people deciding to have children, and parenthood generally implies that everyone shapes the values of one's children in agreement with what they deem valuable. Galston maintains that 'the child is in part (though only in part) an extension of ourselves'[72] and that any attempt to hinder parents' educational efforts in raising their children represents a hateful form of disrespect for parents' expressive liberty.

Liberal states, unlike illiberal regimes that subordinate the parental role in education to the fulfilment of a unitary and homogeneous culture, should respect (obviously within certain limits)[73] expressive liberty and should then agree with the Yoder decision.

---

relates. It would seem that Amish group expressive liberty too (that is, their 'normatively privileged and institutionally defended ability ... to lead their lives as they see fit' [Galston 2005: 45]) is involved in Yoder. In fact, the Amish lament that secular education, by exposing children to an excess of diversity, jeopardizes the perpetuation of their traditional, conservative, agrarian way of life. Some of liberalism's difficulties with the ascription of expressive liberty to groups have been mentioned in Note 20.

[68] Galston (2002a: 102).

[69] A version of this fiduciary model is extensively defended in Arneson and Shapiro (1996).

[70] Galston (2002a: 103).

[71] Galston (2002a: 102). See also Callan (1997).

[72] Galston (2011: 296).

[73] Parents' expressive liberty is an important value but, as Galston (2002a: 102) suggests, 'it is not the only good'. For example, it can neither legitimize ritual

If one considers political pluralism, one can find additional reasons in support of exemption from the last two years of high-school education granted to Amish children by the Yoder decision. As we have seen in the previous section, political pluralism requires that in liberal democracies there be more than one legitimate authority and that state power not be considered the supreme power to which all the others are subordinate. Ian MacMullen claims that Galston's approach to educational policies clearly shows that for him, 'civic goals are not to be privileged over other competing values.'[74] Thus, Yoder, with its recognition that parental authority could be granted a qualified autonomy from the state's educational aspirations, represents a substantial acceptance of the principal tenets of political pluralism.

Amy Gutmann has interpreted Galston's theory as a form of *civic minimalism*, which 'accepts a minimal set of common educational standards but no more. Its aim is to maximize parental authority consistently with keeping a democratic society unified.'[75] The Yoder decision seems acceptable to Galston because Amish people, owing to their peaceful nature and their isolated and agrarian existence, do not constitute a threat to civic peace. In addition, since the Amish can leave their community, they enjoy substantive exit rights.

Here, it should be noted that Galston has a broad conception of exit rights. To have meaningful exit rights, one should be aware of the

---

sacrifice nor exempt parents from responsibilities towards other people and towards institutions. Moreover, parents' expressive liberty should be balanced with children's expressive liberty—which, as they develop, must be given increasing weight.

[74] MacMullen (2007: 45).

[75] Gutmann (2004: 88). A clear statement of Galston's *civic minimalism* is: 'liberal pluralism requires a parsimonious but vigorous system of civic education that teaches tolerance ... and helps equip individuals with the virtues and competences they will need to perform as members of a liberal pluralist economy, society, and polity.' What is required by liberal pluralist system of civic education should not go beyond what is strictly necessary for ensuring 'that the convictions, competences, and virtues required for liberal citizenship are widely shared'. See Galston (2002a: 126–7). Some difficulties encountered by civic minimalism in establishing what is actually required for a working system of civic education have been pointed out by Amy Gutmann; see Gutmann (2004) and the 'Epilogue' to Gutmann (1999: 292–302).

existence of other ways of life, should be able to assess the value of the opportunities one can enjoy outside one's native group, and should possess the capacities needed to participate in another community's life. A further condition for exit rights is that an individual should be free from all the psychological forms of coercion that could hinder her/his normal development.[76] According to Galston, the Amish do not live in a prison as their society meets the requirement of having meaningful exit rights. In fact, young adults become full members of Amish society only if they explicitly accept membership. Further, 'there is no evidence that many former members find themselves unable to cope with the demands of a modern economy and society.'[77] All these considerations work in favour of the acceptance of the legitimacy of (a qualified) parental authority in Yoder.

Galston's agreement with Yoder seems to counter liberal objections according to which Amish people are not good liberal citizens because their 'society is patriarchal—women are regarded as unequal helpers of men—and Amish children are not prepared for being critically receptive citizens'.[78] However, Galston's liberalism, due to the reliance on value pluralism, cannot demand the unquestioned primacy of those political virtues associated with autonomy, rationality, and self-examination. In fact, although the Amish are lacking with regard to autonomy, they can nonetheless score very high with respect to other virtues, such as being law-abiding, responsible, and tolerant of other groups' lifestyles—virtues that are fundamental for a well-functioning liberal democratic society.[79] It is just the acceptance of value pluralism that leads us to reject the claim that in liberal states, compulsory education should be aimed at preparing children for an autonomous and self-examined life. If value pluralism holds, we can question the Socratic notion (accepted more or less tacitly by most of the liberal democratic tradition), according to which 'the unexamined life is an unworthy life, that individual freedom is incompatible with ways of life guided by unquestioned authority or unswerving faith.'[80] Galston thinks that there is still moral goodness outside the

---

[76] Galston (2002a: 123).

[77] Galston (2002a: 106).

[78] Macedo (1995a: 488).

[79] For an extensive discussion of Galston's view on liberal virtues, see Galston (1988, 1991: Chapter 10).

[80] Galston (1989: 99).

narrow domain of autonomy, and Yoder concurs. This is one of the main reasons why Yoder has been rightly decided.

Questioning Diversity Liberalism

Having looked at Galston's liberal theory in many of its relevant aspects, I can proceed to a critical evaluation of his proposal. First, I will argue that Galston misrepresents, both conceptually and historically, the theory he names autonomy liberalism. In so doing, criticizing autonomy liberalism becomes an easier task. Then, I will proceed to a critical evaluation of Galston's diversity liberalism. Some critical remarks will focus on the assumption that the protection of diversity is the starting point for diversity liberalism. After that, I will consider the possibility that value pluralism (which is a view about goods) could slide into a view about plurality of cultures, and the lack of conceptual clarity of a theory that aspires both to comprehensiveness (with its reliance on value pluralism) and to minimal commitments (with its emphasis on the minimal character of negative liberty). Finally, I will account for some problems in Galston's understanding of exit rights, and show that the substantive way in which he accounts for them requires a reliance on autonomy that ends up being inconsistent with the main commitments of Galston's theory.

To begin with, Galston's presentation of autonomy (or Enlightenment) liberalism as a theory committed to promoting autonomy—understood as an individual capacity for rational self-direction—is far from accurate, theoretically and historically. In Emily Gill's *Becoming Free*, one reads that, for Galston, 'a liberal society or government that values and tries to inculcate the capacity for autonomy in all citizens does not promote diversity but undermines it.'[81] What does promoting 'Socratic or Millian ideals as valid for all citizens'[82] mean? Is it true that the advocates of this form of liberalism want actively to encourage the value of autonomy? How is it possible to uphold autonomy without betraying other fundamental liberal premises? Take, for example, Mill, whom Galston considers one of the pre-eminent autonomy liberals. Notwithstanding the perfectionist character of his utilitarian liberalism[83] and his views on the cultivation

---

[81] Gill (2001: 223).
[82] Galston (2002a: 62).
[83] See Donatelli (2006a, 2006b).

of individuality, Mill never argued in favour of public coercive measures aimed at shaping individual character. In fact, Mill remarked that the state should not be directly concerned with the education of children.

As Brian Barry has observed, for Mill (as well as for other autonomy liberals), the role of institutions is to 'provide the conditions under which autonomy can flourish' but not to 'do anything directly to bring about the "ideal of autonomy"'.[84] As discussed in the previous chapter, even Kymlicka, who explicitly endorses autonomy liberalism, distinguishes between the identification of the most appropriate liberal theory and the imposition of that same theory on minorities whose beliefs and world views are not autonomy-oriented. In other words, accepting a liberal theory in which autonomy is the main value does not necessarily commit the majority group to the imposition of autonomous lifestyles on traditional communities and their members.[85]

No liberal society can require that everyone should be engaged in Socratic self-examination, for such an imposition would result in terrible violations of fundamental and traditional liberal guarantees, such as respect for privacy and individuality. Liberal institutional commitments stop at the point where everyone is free to pursue her/his life plan, regardless of whether such plan is inspired by autonomy or by some more traditional ideal.

Furthermore (and with these remarks, I wish to point to the historical inaccuracy mentioned earlier), Galston gives us too-narrow a characterization of Enlightenment liberalism. It is equated with only one Enlightenment strand, that is, the rationalist, according to which 'individual autonomy is identified with the individual exercise of reason, so principles of justice must be constructed which are acceptable to all on the basis of reason alone.'[86] There is another (albeit not dominant in contemporary liberal debate) tradition in Enlightenment that is not considered by Galston: sentimentalism, represented principally by David Hume and Adam Smith, which gave a complex and sophisticated account

---

[84] Barry (2001: 121).

[85] See Kymlicka (1995: 164).

[86] Frazer (2007: 758). More recently, John William Tate has raised some doubts on Galston's distinction between autonomy and diversity liberalism. Tate argues that Locke, Kant, and Mill, counted by Galston among the autonomy liberals, are much more sensitive to diversity than Galston admits. See Tate (2013: 1–18).

of ethics and politics, in which political principles must be endorsed not in terms of reason alone but also in terms of sentiment and emotion.

As far as diversity liberalism is concerned, I would like to argue that it is not clear whether it conceives of diversity as 'its point of departure'[87] or as the value that should be protected or pursued through public policies. To be fair, Galston has acknowledged that 'state authority does not stand under an affirmative obligation to promote diversity.'[88] Nonetheless, it is difficult to underestimate the centrality attributed by Galston to notions such as 'policy of maximum feasible accommodation'[89] and liberalism as protection of diversity. Both these concepts seem to entail some active duties of the state in enhancing diversity. Thus, it is worth restating what has been said in the first chapter, that is, diversity, from a liberal point of view, is a fact of social life having as such no particular value in itself. It is simply a sociological fact that our societies are diverse in terms of morality, religion, and politics. Diversity in itself is not a value, and we can have circumstances in which homogeneity is preferable to diversity. Think, for instance, of the degree of convergence required by some religious or political associations in order to function well. As Chandran Kukathas clearly writes, 'diversity is not the value liberalism pursues but the source of the problem to which it offers a solution.'[90] Liberalism's task is to elaborate agreeable principles that make peaceful coexistence possible in a society pervaded by conflict over the question of how one should live. Thus, those who, like Galston, insist that diversity is the chief value that liberalism should protect confound a factual condition that liberalism is called to face with an end to be pursued.

Another objection that can be formulated against Galston's theory relates to the ways in which value pluralism is employed. This is a view about the plurality and incommensurability of conflicting goods, not cultures. Thus, value pluralism should emphasize a state of affairs in which many values are in a state of potential conflict, but no-priority rule is available to resolve such clashes once they become actual. Galston himself recognizes this feature of value pluralism when he refers to it as a resource upon which liberal theory relies, for he claims that 'while liberal

---

[87] Galston (2002a: 26).
[88] Galston (2004: 145).
[89] Galston (2002a: 20).
[90] Kukathas (2003: 29).

pluralists celebrate legitimate diversity among cultures, they suspect that diversity will exist within culture as well and that a culture's smoothly homogeneous public face reflects the covert operation of power.'[91] This statement, however, is in patent tension with the acceptance of the Amish's restrictions on their children's education because the homogeneity and social immobility of Amish society could be signalling an unjustified and oppressive power exercised by the strongest members of the group against the weakest.

In this regard, I agree with Crowder when he notices that 'Galston does not go as far as Gray in identifying the incommensurability of values with the incommensurability of political regimes, but he tends similarly to equate diversity of goods with diversity of cultures.'[92] If the identification of the incommensurability of values with the incommensurability of political regimes results in a relativistic view, according to which there is no prospect of criticizing political institutions from the outside, even the more moderate equation of diversity of goods with diversity of cultures is a dangerous move towards a relativistic position. This move is both unavailable to Galston, given his oft-stated opinion that 'pluralism is not the same as relativism',[93] and potentially illiberal. In fact, the emphasis on the diversity of cultures might hide the presence of oppression and coerced homogeneity within the groups themselves. It is very likely that there will be conflicts between diversity *among* cultures and *within* cultures, and Galston's theory does not give us clear advice on how to deal with them.

Another critical comment concerns the comprehensive character of Galston's diversity liberalism. At the end of the section, 'Sources of Liberal Theory and Galston's Liberal Pluralism', I observed that Galston wants to remind readers about his distance from political liberalism. His commitment to value pluralism and his objections to the constraints imposed by the norms of public reason on both public life and public discussion would seem sufficient to place Galston firmly in the comprehensive camp. However, the issue is not as simple as it appears at first sight. Some commentators like Kymlicka and Talisse consider Galston a political liberal. In a book published in 1995—that

---

[91] Galston (2002a: 64).
[92] Crowder (2004: 163).
[93] Galston (2002a: 30, 2005: 11).

is, before the publication of the works of Galston that I am considering here—Kymlicka includes Galston among political (or *pro-toleration*, or *pro-diversity*) liberals, such as John Rawls, Charles Larmore, and Donald Moon.[94] Their theories share a common opposition to the commitment to autonomy as the fundamental liberal value[95] for accommodating the claims of groups and individuals who are not properly liberal. An account of Galston as a political liberal is profoundly misconceived because Kymlicka,[96] as is more extensively argued in the first chapter of this book, conflates the *political/comprehensive distinction*, which is about the justification of a liberal theory, with *pro-autonomy/pro-diversity distinction*, which is about the value that a liberal theory might assume as fundamental.

Talisse, instead, challenges the view that diversity liberalism is a comprehensive theory.[97] Galston's appeal regarding the relevance of the presumption against coercion and in favour of negative liberty would render his liberal pluralism dangerously akin to Rawlsian political liberalism.[98] Given that the presumption against coercion and the primacy of negative liberty, understood along value pluralist lines, would be a widespread view in a liberal society, it seems that Galston agrees with one of the three features commonly ascribed to political liberalism (namely, that political principles are to be worked out starting from what Rawls calls the 'implicitly recognized basic ideas and principles'[99] of a liberal democratic society). This objection has already been discussed and I argued that Galston's reliance on negative liberty and on the idea that coercion always should be justified is not an arbitrary assumption of a default position, but rather a consequence of the acceptance of value pluralism as the most 'adequate' view about ethics.

There is still another consideration that may blur the distinction between Galston's theory and political liberalism, and that is his

---

[94] See Kymlicka (1995).

[95] See as illustrative examples of their ideas, Larmore (1987), Moon (1993), and Rawls (2005).

[96] Kymlicka (1995: 158). He continues to consider Galston a political liberal in one of his later works too; see Kymlicka (2002).

[97] Talisse (2004: 136).

[98] I say 'dangerously' because that proximity is against the author's declared purposes.

[99] Rawls (2005: 8). See Chapter 1.

understanding of negative liberty as a very minimal notion that is independent of disputable philosophical and metaphysical assumptions. Such an idea would work as the basis of a liberal theory thought of as a *minimal moral conception*,[100] indistinguishable from political liberalism with its search for a consensus on some shared basic values as a guarantee of a just and stable political society.

Thus, it would seem that Galston's search for a minimal[101] notion of negative liberty might convert his diversity liberalism into a *political* theory. And yet, Galston's reliance on value pluralism is too fundamental to be disregarded as the main factor that renders his theory a comprehensive liberalism. Galston himself remains faithful to it even when it leads him to endorse conclusions that are, in some respects, not compatible with central tenets of liberal political morality. For instance, in the discussion of Yoder, I observed that the employment of value pluralism as one of the resources of diversity liberalism works as an instrument for giving priority to diversity and for explaining that autonomy and self-examination are not the only virtues liberalism should care for.

To conclude, I will briefly consider the way in which exit rights are understood by Galston, and evaluate the trouble they can create for diversity liberalism. As we have seen in the preceding section, Galston's view of exit rights is quite demanding and goes well beyond a merely formal view, according to which an individual is free to separate from the group to which s/he belongs when the group neither erects formal barriers nor practices any physical coercion preventing the dissociation. It seems, however, that if someone meets all the conditions listed in Galston's book, *Liberal Pluralism*,[102] the distinction between autonomy

---

[100] This is political liberalism in Larmore's understanding. See Larmore (1996: 133).

[101] And, due to this minimalism, potentially shareable by everybody.

[102] In this book, Galston (2002a: 123) maintains:

A meaningful right would seem to include at least the following elements: *knowledge conditions*—the awareness of alternatives to the life one is in fact living; *capacity conditions*—the ability to assess these alternatives if it comes to seem desirable to do so; *psychological conditions*—in particular, freedom from the kinds of brainwashing that give rise to heartrending deprogramming efforts of parents on behalf of their children, and more broadly, forms of coercion other than the purely physical that may give rise to warranted state interference on behalf of affected individuals; and finally, *fitness conditions*—the ability of

and diversity liberalism fades away. As Crowder has argued, 'real free-dom of exit seems to involve the capacity to stand back from the group's norms and to assess them critically—that is, the capacity for autonomous judgement.'[103] Thus, in the light of these considerations on the exit rights issue, it would seem that there is no authentic difference between Galston's view and the more demanding Enlightenment liberalism that relies on allegedly sectarian individual autonomy.

In other words, the exit rights discourse pushes Galston's diversity liberalism towards a dilemma. A weak and formal conception of exit rights makes diversity liberalism insensitive to the rights of the weakest members of the groups, insofar as a merely formal freedom to dissociate would leave the weakest in the group at the mercy of the most powerful. Think, for instance, of a poor and illiterate woman born and raised within a conservative, patriarchal society. She could be formally free to leave, in the sense that no physical impediments are put in her way. She may not, however, be aware of the opportunities that she could enjoy outside her native community. She may also lack the psychological and economic capacities needed for leaving an abusive husband. Could one conclude that she has a real opportunity to leave and to emancipate herself from the oppressive practices of her group? On the other hand, a strong version of exit rights would either undermine the distinction between diversity and autonomy liberalism[104] or lead the former to collapse into the latter.[105] It must be said that Galston is well aware of this dilemma and, in *The Practice of Liberal Pluralism*, mentions the possibility of distinguishing between an objectionable 'Socratic/Millian ideal of autonomy' and a more acceptable 'more modest conception of autonomy as freedom of choice'.[106] He never elaborates on this distinction, however, and the problem persists.

To conclude, Galston's liberalism has been submitted to a series of objections that raise serious doubts about its theoretical consistency and adequacy as a theoretical tool for dealing with diversity. The promising

---

exit-desiring individuals to participate effectively in at least some ways of life other than the ones they wish to leave.

[103] Crowder (2007: 128).
[104] Weinstock (2008).
[105] Crowder (2013: 162).
[106] Galston (2005: 182).

reliance on diversity and the objections to autonomy liberalism are not enough to make this a tenable conception. Our search for a viable liberal conception has to build on this pro-diversity character, but, at the same time, has to avoid all the difficulties noticed in Galston's theory. As the next chapter will show, the politicization of liberalism—putting aside all the controversies created by the commitment to value pluralism—will be fundamental to our theoretical enterprise.

4

Political Liberalism and Diversity

The Limits of Political Transformations

This chapter engages in the way in which PA liberalism deals with diversity. Stephen Macedo's work[1] is assumed as an illustration of this kind of theory. In Macedo's view, the politicization of liberalism coexists with a commitment to the value of autonomy, although the autonomy that political liberalism refers to is, as it will appear clearer in the following pages, a political notion.

Macedo's politicization of liberal theory can be understood as a progress beyond the weakness of comprehensive liberalisms' attempts to accommodate diversity that has already been analysed in Chapters 2 and 3. Political liberalism is mainly a Rawlsian idea, and Macedo's position is overtly relying on John Rawls's thoughts.[2] Nevertheless, his theory has some noteworthy peculiarities that make it independent from the original Rawlsian formulation. Above all, Macedo is more candid than Rawls about liberal partisanship and the impossibility of achieving a completely neutral justification for a liberal theory. However, I would like to point out here that Macedo does not completely reject the liberal value of neutrality. Rather, as this chapter will show, he argues for a very constrained notion

---

[1] Macedo (2000a).
[2] See especially Rawls (2005).

of neutrality, allegedly consistent with the ambitions and structure of political liberalism.

Macedo's theory is also characterized by a noticeable civic dimension. The idea is that, in order to flourish, liberal societies need a civic life of a certain kind. Citizens must be educated so that they can contribute to the thriving of liberal order. This means, among other things, that a liberalism such as Macedo's cannot accept diversity as having value per se. This form of liberalism, in fact, distinguishes between healthy and unhealthy forms of diversity, and argues in favour of transforming collective and individual identities so that they can actively support the liberal society.

It is this view of transformation, as I will argue, that is problematic. As I have observed earlier, the concept of transformation of groups' identities is not tricky as such. In Chapter 2, Will Kymlicka's view has been critiqued for the narrowness of the notion of comprehensive autonomy according to which the transformations are to be conducted. In the case of Macedo, problems do not disappear despite the fact that the notion of autonomy to which the theory appeals is less substantive and divisive. In fact, it is just the emphasis on the political notion of autonomy and the request by PA liberalism that individuals become politically autonomous that does not allow this approach to show adequate respect to minority groups.

The chapter is divided into different sections. In the section that follows, the politicization of liberalism will be analysed and considered as a step that liberalism needs to accomplish in order to be more accommodative towards normative diversity. The next section deals with the strong civic dimension of PA liberalism and shows how it works in accounting for the process of transformation of identities when the inclusion of minorities is at stake. The following section explains the role neutrality plays within PA liberalism. I argue that, despite its alleged neutrality, PA liberalism ends up promoting autonomy, although this autonomy is a political value. In the penultimate section, I will discuss educational policies as a domain in which the fact that PA liberalism promotes autonomy is particularly evident. Finally, the last section articulates some critical remarks on PA liberalism on the basis of its failure to consider the consequences of inclusion of minorities in a society that aims at being faithful to liberal principles in a proper way. I argue that although PA liberalism grasps a fundamental aspect of liberalism (that is, individual and collective identities must be shaped in specific ways to be supportive of liberal

order) that is often neglected in contemporary literature, the aim of transformative mechanisms (a society in which individuals become *politically
autonomous*) is excessively narrow and does not adequately address the
concerns of those minorities that are asking for accommodation in liberal
democratic societies.

The Politicization of Liberalism

Macedo's work is a clear expression of the precepts of political liberalism. In a 1995 article about the problems posed to liberal civic education by moral and religious pluralism, Macedo objects to comprehensive
liberalisms on the basis that their ideals are 'deeply partisan and not
easily defended' and that they 'claim too much'.[3] Given the persistence of
disagreement among reasonable individuals on the ultimate matters of
ethics, religion, and philosophy,[4] and given that homogeneity about these
controversial matters is either unfeasible or achievable only through an
intolerably intrusive use of state coercion, political authority should not
be premised on the validity of divisive comprehensive doctrines. For
instance, the view that critical thinking is a necessary feature of a good
life, or that religious truths are to be achieved or known in some specific
ways, is unlikely to work as the foundation of our collective life.

Macedo's politicization of liberalism closely follows Rawls's approach
in *Political Liberalism*.[5] Macedo proposes to bracket some divisive issues,
such as religious beliefs or the ideals that contribute to the realization
of a perfectly good human life. In this approach, the justification of 'at
least the most basic matters of justice' is not limited to those citizens
who share our peculiar view of the whole meaning of life. In fact,
political liberalism aims at justifying fundamental matters of justice 'on
grounds widely acceptable to reasonable people'.[6] In the Rawlsian jargon,

---

[3] Macedo (1995a: 473).

[4] This is the so-called 'fact of reasonable pluralism'. As Rawls (2005: xvi)
argues, '[P]olitical liberalism assumes that a plurality of reasonable yet incom-
patible comprehensive doctrines is the normal result of the exercise of human
reason within the framework of the free institutions of a constitutional democratic
regime.'

[5] Rawls (2005).

[6] Macedo (1995a: 473).

reasonable people are those who 'are prepared to offer one another fair terms of social cooperation' and 'agree to act on those terms, even at the cost of their own interests in particular situations, provided that others also accept those terms'.[7] The notion of reasonableness is so crucial in Macedo's work that 'the desire to respect reasonable people'[8] is the core motive of his political liberalism.

According to Macedo as well as Rawls, political liberalism requires that when individuals 'bracket' their deepest convictions, they have to focus upon what reasonable people can share notwithstanding their deep disagreements. One could say that, contrary to comprehensive liberals who pursue what could be called 'a strategy of engagement' (in the sense that they bring on the political scene the disagreements on fundamental matters so that they can be dealt with directly),[9] political liberals practise a much more modest 'strategy of avoidance' aimed at getting a fair agreement. The underlying idea is that 'citizens who disagree about their highest ideals and their conceptions of the whole truth can nevertheless agree on public aims such as securing the equal enjoyment of a broad array of freedoms, establishing democratic institutions, and providing a basic social safety net.'[10] This agreement, political liberals contend, can be reached without a shared specific comprehensive account of ethics, religion, and metaphysics.

It is noteworthy that the theory Macedo defends is not sceptical. His theory is not led by the idea that human reason is unfit to know moral, religious, or other metaphysical truths. Macedo is extremely clear in maintaining that even if 'political liberalism does not assert a particular view of the truth',[11] that does not amount to saying that no truth is identifiable when we consider fundamental concerns. What is relevant from a political liberal perspective is the acknowledgement of the difficulty of reaching a public agreement on a comprehensive set of values.[12]

---

[7] Rawls (2005: xlii).

[8] Macedo (2000a: 170).

[9] Macedo (1995a: 491).

[10] Macedo (2000a: 170).

[11] Macedo (2000a: 197).

[12] In an article, Macedo (1995b: 307) writes:

Political liberalism does not stand for scepticism about ultimate questions of moral and religious truth. Scepticism is a particular account of the nature of

Political liberalism does not demand that individuals have to be indifferent towards their religious affiliations or their other, ultimate ethical commitments even in their private lives. Political liberalism assumes that each individual has her/his own comprehensive doctrine and that s/he can relate it to the political domain, which is defined by what reasonable people can share, according to their own interpretations.[13] However, the primacy of the political domain only holds when matters of particular relevance are at stake. In fact, political liberals argue that the appeal to comprehensive doctrines is suspicious only when a society is fashioning 'basic principles of justice',[14] that is, those fundamental rights and political principles that direct the coercive powers of the state. In other, less significant circumstances, every individual can lead her/his life according to the demands of her/his comprehensive doctrine.

The politicization of liberalism can be understood as a tool for amending the narrowness of comprehensive liberalism in accommodating and accounting for the problem of diversity. In fact, as Macedo maintains in a 1998 article, political liberalism is to be preferred to its opponent because it, almost as a definitional matter, 'accommodates a greater *philosophical diversity* at the foundational level than comprehensive versions of liberalism'.[15] If political liberalism's justification of the political order does not rely on the validity of one among many conflicting conceptions of the good, it can more fairly accommodate and acknowledge the so-called 'fact of reasonable pluralism'. Political liberalism neither takes a position on ultimate matters that are not directly relevant in the political domain

---

such claim: namely, that none of them is true. Political liberalism does not deny that there is a true view, it insists only that a democratic policy should attempt to respect the many reasonable views about the good life that citizens espouse.

[13] Macedo (2000a: 190) writes:

[C]omprehensive religious and moral conceptions are regarded as inappropriate grounds for determining the shape of basic political institutions (because these conceptions are sources of reasonable disagreements). But that does not mean that what has been put aside is valueless or irrelevant to individual citizens. Quite the contrary, much of value is outside of the shared grounds of a liberal public morality.

[14] Macedo (2000a: 177).

[15] Macedo (1998: 79); emphasis added.

nor confers any priority to some lifestyles and values they depend upon. On the contrary, a comprehensive liberalism that assumes autonomy as its core value 'does not show very much respect for the choices citizens may make to live nonautonomously, as members of hierarchical societies or corporate bodies'.[16] Thus, political liberalism has to be preferred since it neither privileges those who, for instance, are committed to an autonomy-inspired conception of the good life, nor marginalizes those who conceive their flourishing within the path endorsed by some conservative religious communities.

It has to be remarked that the openness of political liberalism towards diversity operates at the philosophical level. As Macedo shows,[17] political liberalism, given its freestandingness, scores higher than comprehensive liberalism in accommodating a more elevated degree of (reasonable) philosophical diversity. The diversity that is *actually* accommodated is a further matter, and Macedo's political liberalism is quite far from a simple laissez-faire approach towards diversity. In fact, as the following sections show, his theory does not stand either for an unconstrained neutrality among different conceptions of the good or for an undifferentiated acceptance of diversity.

The Civic and Transformative Dimensions of Political Liberalism

Macedo's political liberalism differs from those political theories that celebrate plurality and difference as such. He is critical of those theorists who *romantically*[18] celebrate diversity in itself and think that a more diverse society is to be always pursued as a suitable end for public policies. Macedo thinks that 'diversity needs to be kept in its place: diversity is not always a value and it should not be accepted uncritically.'[19] Even for political liberalism, there are 'healthy' and 'unhealthy' forms of diversity, and the purpose of a sound political theory is to distinguish

---

[16] Nussbaum (1999: 110).

[17] Macedo (1998).

[18] Macedo (1995a: 489). Here, Macedo mainly refers to William Galston's discussion of educational policies for children from conservative religious minorities, such as the Amish. See Galston (1995).

[19] Macedo (2000a: 3).

between diversities that should be accommodated and those that should be rejected, restrained, or somehow deterred.

The liberalism advocated by Macedo is pretty demanding. According to him, liberal societies are founded on 'shared political commitments' rather than on diversity. Keeping alive a thriving liberal society requires 'a shared public morality'[20] and specific citizens' virtues that are not natural but demand public intervention. The intervention should primarily be in the state educational system, but it can also be extended through other less direct means. Roughly stated, given that a liberal society is possible only if its individuals become good citizens and given that 'there is no reason to think that the dispositions that characterize good liberal citizens come about naturally',[21] the state should act in order to create the conditions of its own perpetuation.

These remarks seem enough to indicate that Macedo objects to what he labels 'liberal legalism'.[22] This latter is the view according to which law is simply a system of impartial rules constituting the framework within which individuals and groups pursue their different and potentially conflicting ends. In liberal legalism, law is purposeless and the main function of the government is to enforce law and regulate the likely conflicts of interest that might arise among individuals and groups. Liberal legalism is valuable insofar as it helps to account for the fact that law assures ordered liberty and allows individuals and groups to pursue, in peaceful ways, their aims. However, for Macedo, liberal legalism should be rejected since it does not account for 'some of the deepest ambitions of a liberal constitutional order'.[23]

Liberalism, Macedo contends, has a *transformative* dimension that one cannot grasp if one stops at the tenets of liberal legalism. As mentioned earlier, liberal societies' flourishing is not a natural fact but depends on citizens' attitudes and dispositions that are neither spontaneous nor self-sustaining. A liberal state needs to *transform* individuals' and groups' commitments so that they can actively support liberal order. Active support is more than mere acquiescence to the coercive power of liberal institutions.

---

[20] Macedo (2000a: 146).

[21] Macedo (2000a: 16).

[22] Macedo (1998: 57).

[23] Macedo (1998: 57).

Since his first monograph,[24] Macedo has distinguished between two ways of living in a liberal regime. First, there is *liberal coexistence*. In this case, we have an outward conformity to liberal institutions that can coexist with reciprocal indifference (or even hostility), joined with common fear of punishment for the violations of liberal rules. Liberal coexistence is the primitive way of affirming liberalism and of living according to liberal norms and institutions. It is characteristic of the period in which liberal tolerance emerged as a pragmatic tool for accommodating religious pluralism, after religious wars in the seventeenth century. However, liberal coexistence is not the only and not 'the best way of affirming liberal justice'.[25] Liberalism can be more than a modus vivendi and citizens can actively support liberal justice for moral reasons. This second way of living, according to the principles of liberalism, is possible when individuals affirm liberal justice critically and reflectively.

Macedo points out that the interest in the ways in which individuals and communities support the political order is not alien to the history of liberal thought. Rather, it is an old concern, in spite of those who think that liberalism is an atomistic theory concerned only with the respect of individual rights.[26] For instance, a classical liberal such as Adam Smith was aware that 'local communities and other intermediate associations are important indirect instruments of civic education',[27] which the state can shape and manage through public policies so that they can become supportive of liberal democracy.

Thus, from the perspective of Macedo's political liberalism, healthy forms of diversity are those which are 'supportive of basic principles of justice'.[28] To flourish in suitable ways, liberal state has to constitute normative diversity for its own ends. Collective and individual identities need to be transformed so that they become able to hold up a liberal democratic society. The process through which American Catholic Church was liberalized in the 1960s and, after a long period of distrust and suspicion, became a vigorous supporter of democracy around the world is

---

[24] Macedo (1990).

[25] Macedo (1990: 254–5).

[26] These objections to liberal theory have been formulated, for instance, by Taylor (1985).

[27] Macedo (1996: 252).

[28] Macedo (2000a: 134).

assumed as an illustration of the 'transformative potential' of liberalism. Macedo remarks that this transformation was not a mere chance event. The change was the deliberate outcome of, among other political acts, the principle of a secular political environment in which political and religious power are separated.

Macedo's liberalism emphasizes the state role in shaping normative diversity and the fact that the civil society it envisages is a shared moral space in which citizens respect one another as equal participants in the collective enterprise of self-government. It is for these reasons that Macedo's theory seems to go well beyond political liberalism's basic concerns with fundamental constitutional principles. According to Macedo himself, his theory is a kind of *civic* liberalism that emphasizes both the educative ambitions of liberalism and the significance of a broad civic life.[29] For him, in fact, 'liberalism has an important civic dimension: it proposes not simply a set of negative mechanisms for limiting and controlling political power, but also includes positive means for fostering a politics worthy of esteem.'[30] If this is so, one could ask: What is the difference between this sort of political liberalism and other comprehensive liberalisms that stress upon the relevance of civic virtues or other more explicitly republican approaches? Is Macedo's political liberalism nothing more than a veiled form of comprehensive liberalism, as some of his critics have claimed?[31]

According to Macedo, what distinguishes political liberalism from comprehensive liberalism is the fact that, according to the former, the justification of the constraints imposed on acceptable diversity does not go beyond what is shared by different comprehensive positions. The main difference between the two versions of liberal theory resides in the way in which they defend the constraints to the admissible diversity: 'political liberalism stands for a measure of restraint that would be unnatural for one committed to a vision of the good life as a whole informed by autonomy or individuality.'[32] In other words, the more one is committed to substantive ideals, the less s/he will accept restraints on her/his attempt to shape public institutions according to these same views.

[29] Macedo (2000a: 169).
[30] Macedo (2000b: 14).
[31] Dostert (2006: 46) and Wolfe (2006: 116).
[32] Macedo (2000a: 175).

Despite these cautious distinctions, Macedo's liberalism is unapologetically transformative up to the point that it does not even despise assimilation, provided that it operates in non-oppressive ways and is directed towards justifiable values, which are those that can be defended without an appeal to comprehensive doctrines. In fact, as Macedo argues, '[T]he point of the transformative mechanisms is political. They are deployed in liberal politics, and their effects are welcomed insofar as they secure a system of political liberty and other basic political goods.'[33] Liberal transformations stress the need to enhance our civil interests— the common interests of citizens who decide to peacefully live together in a free and diverse society—and not to advance, for instance, a religion over another religion or atheism over other religious beliefs. In this sense, Macedo's view is less demanding and more open to diversity than, for instance, John Dewey's *civic totalism*, with his idea that civic engagement is overwhelmingly relevant and that democratic public morality should be concerned with what is ultimately true. Moreover, political liberalism is not grounded in a pro-science comprehensive view that is opposed to religious beliefs as such.[34]

Thus, political liberalism neither has a negative attitude towards religious beliefs as such (or towards other, different particular loyalties), nor does it want, in a Deweyan spirit, 'to dissolve traditional religions in order to transfer religious energies to the common political project of progressive reform and the advancement of science and culture'.[35] It only requires that religious and other groups transform in a civic direction, so that they are supportive of the liberal institutions.

Political Liberalism, Neutrality, and Public Justification

Considering the arguments presented till now, it would seem that neutrality does not have a significant place in Macedo's political liberalism. Neutrality, as Kymlicka has argued, is the view that 'the state should not reward or penalize particular conceptions of the good life but, rather, should provide a neutral framework within which different and

---

[33] Macedo (2000a: 137).
[34] See Dewey (1923, 1934).
[35] Macedo (2000a: 139–40).

potentially conflicting conceptions of the good can be pursued.'[36] If one accepts this definition, then one could say that arguing in favour of transforming individual and collective identities to support liberal order is far from neutral. In fact, some conceptions of the good, especially those passing through a considerable process of change, will be penalized. Others will not be at ease in a social environment as envisaged by political liberal principles.

These considerations are not particularly relevant for Macedo's views and for political liberalism in general. They would be crucial if the neutrality Macedo's theory is looking for was consequential neutrality,[37] which is neutrality related to the outcomes of public policies. However, Macedo's political liberalism does not demand that laws, institutions, and collective decisions must have the same consequences for all the conceptions of the good that happen to be present in a liberal democratic society. It is unavoidable that different conceptions will be differently affected by the framework constituted by liberal rights and freedoms.[38] For instance, in a society that universally enforces and protects universal rights, those groups who do not recognize women's rights will suffer greater limitations on their conduct than those for whom equality between sexes is a condition that cannot be renounced.

Political liberalism aims at *justificatory* neutrality. Macedo is extremely clear about liberal partisanship and on the fact that political liberalism is not an exception to the thought that any justification is contentious. He claims that neutrality has to be understood only in the limited sense that 'liberal political values (at least those that undergird the constitutional essentials and matters of basic justice) should not depend upon particular religious and (what John Rawls called) comprehensive philosophical worldviews.'[39] This is, for sure, a very constrained notion of neutrality whose operation can be better understood if one considers the idea of public justification.

---

[36] Kymlicka (1989b: 883). Neutral liberalism in this sense is defended, among the others, by Ackerman (1980) and Dworkin (1978).

[37] Kymlicka (1989b: 884). For a more recent account of the meaning of liberal neutrality, see Patten (2012).

[38] For Rawls's rejection of consequential neutrality, see Rawls (2005: 193, 195–200).

[39] Macedo (2010: 24); author's translation.

According to Macedo, liberalism is not only a theory focused on individual rights, guarantees, and liberties, but also on the idea of public justification. In fact, he approvingly quotes Jeremy Waldron's view that 'liberals demand that the social order should in principle be capable of explaining itself at the tribunal of each person's understanding.'[40] The essential premise of Macedo's Rawlsian justificatory strategy is that 'public power belongs to us all as fellow citizens, and we should exercise it together based in reasons and arguments we can share in spite of our differences.'[41] The process through which persons give and receive reasons is required in order to give legitimacy to the coercive power exercised by the state on all its citizens. Given the deep disagreements about different, but still reasonable, world views, these reasons have to be *public*, in the sense that they should be independent of what the person perceives as true from the vantage point of her/his own comprehensive doctrine.[42] It is publicity that guarantees that no particular comprehensive view involves the subordination of those persons who, notwithstanding their reasonableness, are committed to other minority comprehensive doctrines. Publicity also ensures the possibility of achieving the fundamental aim of political liberalism, namely, 'a political community of principle in which citizens share not only a common effective authority, but also public moral principles and a mutually acceptable and convincing rationale for those principles'.[43]

The constraints imposed by public justification and public reason[44] have invited objections from non-liberals as well as other liberal thinkers. Critics have focused on several arguments: some of them claim that, at the end of the day, the requirements of public justification and public reason

---

[40] Waldron (1987: 149).

[41] Macedo (2000b: 25). This passage explicitly draws on Rawls's liberal principle of legitimacy. See Rawls (2005: 137).

[42] See Maffettone (2010: Chapter 11).

[43] Macedo (2000a: 178).

[44] Public reason, for Rawlsian liberals, is both 'a standard by which we measure laws and political institutions' and 'a set of guidelines to regulate the behaviour of legislators, judges, and ordinary citizens. Public reason requires a form of deliberative democracy, whereby citizens only support those fundamental laws and political institutions that they sincerely believe can be justified by appeal to political values that others could reasonably accept.' See Quong (2014: 265).

silences some groups, especially religious and conservative ones,[45] or that these requirements hide biases towards conservative moral views; others raise doubts on the difficulty of clearly detaching public from non-public reasons; and some others observe that public reason conceived according to political liberalism's precepts can result in the weakening of the vitality of a healthy public sphere and in the incapacity of publicly pursuing truth.[46]

In a 2010 article, Macedo has attempted to reply to such objections.[47] He has stressed that the main criticisms are misplaced or exaggerated. As a matter of fact, today, even conservative and religious fundamentalists try to fashion their arguments in terms of public reason. This practice is so widespread that it would be strange if, in a political debate, some-one used God's revelation to strengthen her/his arguments. Moreover, the acceptance of the Rawlsian *wide view* of public reason, according to which 'reasonable comprehensive doctrines, religious or nonreligious, may be introduced in public political discussion at any time, provided that in due course proper political reasons are presented',[48] appears to be enough inclusive even for those fearing the exclusionary effects due to public reason. This revised view of public reason does not put particular restrictions on public discussion as such, but only demands that a shared public justification be available when universally binding laws are at stake. However, I will not deal with these complex matters in this chapter. In the following section, my analysis will focus on the so-called *spillover effects* of this form of liberalism of public reason. Hereafter, I will consider public educational policies as a domain in which these spillover effects are particularly noticeable. Education is particularly relevant for Macedo's liberalism since it is a field of public policy in which normative diversity is more perceptibly transformed for civic purposes.

Political Liberalism and the Promotion of Political Autonomy

In the previous sections, I have shown that Macedo's political liberalism does not defend neutrality of effects and that it requires a transformation

---

[45] Fish (1999).

[46] Raz (1990).

[47] Macedo (2010).

[48] Rawls (2005: 462). This idea is presented for the first time in Rawls (1997). This article has been included in Rawls (2005), from which I am quoting.

of individual and collective identities so that they can support liberal order. The transformative potential of political liberalism is particularly relevant when public education is at stake. In fact, education copes with children, namely, with persons who temporarily are less than full citizens and can be shaped according to the plans of the educational system. Civic-spirited public school, in Macedo's views, should aim at promoting the rationality and autonomy of their students. The latter could be shaped to acquire capabilities that can facilitate their choice of lifestyles, independent from their families. In addition, public schools (unlike private religious or secular schools), in general, expose their pupils to an extended diversity of religious, political, and moral beliefs. Some problems can come from the fact that this diversity can clash with the homogeneity required by some conservative groups as a necessary condition for individual and collective thriving.

Macedo claims that 'all children should have an education that provides them with the ability to make informed and independent decisions about how they want to lead their lives in our modern world. Liberal freedoms to choose are the birthright of every child.'[49] In other words, children have to receive an education that enables them to become good liberal citizens who might support liberal order. Macedo admits that if the state promotes some liberal virtues through public schools, such as developing a critical attitude towards competing political or religious claims or the respect for moral and religious pluralism, it will encourage critical thinking in general. In sum, considering that it is difficult to insulate what one learns in the classroom with how one behaves in her/his extra-school life, a spillover of liberal civic virtues into other realms of life is to be expected.[50]

Some considerations on Macedo's position about *Wisconsin v. Yoder*, which I have more extensively discussed in Chapter 3, will be helpful in understanding better the way in which his political/civic liberalism deals with diversity in educational matters. The starting point of Macedo's treatment of the Amish is that, notwithstanding the fact that they are hardworking and peaceful people, they are quite far from being good

---

[49] Macedo (2000a: 207).
[50] Macedo (2000a: 179). The spillover problem of political liberalism has been broadly discussed in Tomasi (2001).

liberal citizens.[51] Their society is patriarchal, and thus not egalitarian as far as gender relations are concerned. Moreover, Amish tradition does not permit that their children be educated to become reflective and civically oriented citizens. Therefore, if one allows Amish parents to directly care for the education of their children, the expected outcome is that the children will not develop their capacities to become good liberal citizens.

According to Macedo, 'that the children are prepared for the life in the Amish community is not enough: it is for the children to say whether that is what they wish.'[52] Amish children, like other pupils from whatever group, should be free to choose whether they want to remain or leave their native communities and join other groups. This choice is possible only when the education they receive makes them able to do so. Thus, granting an exemption from public schools, like the one demanded by Amish parents in *Wisconsin* v. *Yoder*, could involve a severe impairment in children's capabilities to have an open future. This is why, in principle, the exemption should not be granted. Macedo hopes that '*Yoder* remains a "dead end" in American constitutional law'[53] and claims that it should be invalidated.

I think that the intriguing theoretical problem for Macedo, who, as I have argued before, defends a political liberalism that also has a thick civic dimension, is to find a way to combine the rejection of founding liberal theory in comprehensive world views with its explicit civic orientation. It would seem that the more one looks at the way in which public schools shape children's character to make them good liberal citizens (in the sense of self-directing and critical individuals), the more the state betrays its commitment to a comprehensive idea of human flourishing.[54] In this case, the comprehensive ideal could be a Millian theory of individuality, or a Kantian view of autonomy, or any comprehensive account that could possibly be rejected by traditional groups.

[51] Macedo (2000a: 207). With regard to this point, Macedo admittedly relies on Spinner-Halev (1994: 87–108).

[52] Macedo (2000a: 208).

[53] Macedo (2000a: 208). These considerations do not rule out that even justified laws and policies can admit exemptions. When these measures impose 'special burdens' on particular groups and individuals, some exceptions can be granted for reasons of fairness. See Macedo (2010).

[54] A similar doubt has been raised by Wolfe (2006: 116).

In other terms, one can wonder whether the way in which the issue of education is dealt with shows that the distinction between political liberalism and comprehensive liberalism vanishes. Rawls himself admits that, in spite of the great difference in scope and generality between the two forms of liberal theory, there is some resemblance between the values championed by political liberalism and the ones supported by comprehensive liberals such as Kant and Mill.[55] Macedo is well aware of this issue, and specifies that his aim 'is not to promote a comprehensive philosophical doctrine of autonomy or individuality, but to make sure that no authority imposes an intellectual tyranny on children'.[56] Stated differently, the notion of autonomy employed by his approach is limited to the political domain, although it easily spills over in other spheres of life. It is as if Macedo's theory requires that all individuals become *politically* autonomous, and this transformation will also end up in making them *morally* autonomous. *Political* autonomy is, as Rawls has pointed out, 'the legal independence and assured political integrity of citizens and their sharing with other citizens equally in the exercise of political power',[57] whereas *moral* autonomy expresses itself in a life of reflection and critical examination of commitments, ideas, attitudes, and values.

At this point, leaving aside what Macedo has written, one has to consider whether political and moral autonomy are really different and, more generally, whether the distinction between political and moral liberalism collapses. I do not think that political liberalism is nothing more than a disguised comprehensive liberalism. Although their effects might be almost undistinguishable, I contend that there is still a difference between comprehensive and political liberalism. The former is a theory that justifies social order starting from substantive ethical commitments, whereas the latter is a theory that starts from what different and yet reasonable comprehensive world views share. One could say that, analogously, the difference between utilitarianism and rights-based theories still holds

---

[55] Rawls (2005: 200). Abbey and Spinner-Halev (2013) maintain that Rawls's political liberalism and Mill's comprehensive liberalism make use of similar conceptions of autonomy and that a Rawlsian state would be more invasive than a Millian state.

[56] Macedo (2000a: 238).

[57] Rawls (2005: xlii).

even if both can, starting from their own philosophical premises, justify a right to, say, active euthanasia. Even such being the case, one can still object to the 'practical implications'[58] of political liberalism, for example, the kind of society it fosters or the virtues it promotes in direct or indirect ways.

The point on the difference between comprehensive and political liberalism is strengthened if we consider the works of some scholars who have been enquiring on the compatibility between Islam and liberal democratic values. Hamid Haidar, for instance, contends that political liberalism, with its focus on the need to avoid questions connected with the ultimate truth of a set of religious beliefs, tends to be less sectarian than 'deeply secular' and 'truth seeking'[59] comprehensive liberalism. Further, Andrew March has shown that in the case of Muslim minorities, political liberalism can vindicate its aspiration 'to win the support of otherwise nonliberal social groups'.[60] In fact, Muslim citizens would prefer a situation in which their religious and metaphysical beliefs can be politically expressed. However, given that the political power is shared with non-Muslims citizens in the public arena, it would be desirable to ground political power on the shared aspects of different comprehensive doctrines (as political liberalism requires). In fact, Muslims could have some difficulties in conceiving themselves as full citizens if non-Muslim states advance some metaphysical claims that are opposite to what they sincerely believe.[61]

---

[58] Tomasi (2001: 9). In the book, Tomasi (2001: 10) argues that political liberalism can be objected for its 'sociological effects' even if 'the form of justification sought by political liberals *succeeds*'. Tomasi's leading idea is that a theory can be correctly justified and yet its effects can be objectionable. In the case of political liberalism, the reasons for objections concern the fact that in a society ruled by its principles not all the conceptions of the good will be equally affected. This means that, as a consequence of political liberalism, the conditions of some conception of the good will improve, whereas for other conceptions of the good, the situation will be made worse.

[59] Haidar (2008: 104). Haidar considers Rawls and Mill as examples of (respectively) political and comprehensive liberalism. In this case, the reflections on Rawls hold for Macedo too, given his explicit reliance on Rawlsian ideas.

[60] March (2007: 250); see also March (2006).

[61] March (2007: 250).

The Narrowness of Political Transformations

Up till now, the reconstruction of Macedo's thought has been persuasive in demonstrating that the politicization of liberalism represents a
fascinating theoretical move for accommodating diversity. I have argued
beforehand that political liberalism scores higher than comprehensive
liberalism in the accommodation of 'philosophical diversity at the foundational level'.[62] Eschewing any appeal to ultimate truths and focusing on
the political domain (although it is not seen as isolated from other extra-
political concerns), political liberalism can claim the allegiance of many
who would not feel comfortable in a society governed by comprehensive
liberalism.

In addition, Macedo's approach, with its emphasis on the civic dimension of political liberalism, enables us to grasp the fundamental dimension of the transformation of individual and collective identities involved
in the process of accommodation of diversity. Nonetheless, as I contend
in the remaining part of this section, Macedo's understanding of the
transformative dimension of liberalism is misleading and incomplete.

In a passage that addresses the problem of groups that are worthy
of being accommodated, Macedo writes that 'the important point is that
we must decide which communities are to be accommodated, and that
there is nothing wrong with deciding on the basis of the best reasons
that are available, and with due confidence in the worth of preserving
liberal institutions.'[63] Nonetheless, conceding this point, namely, that *we*
have the duty to decide whom and according to which principles groups
and individuals are to be included in *our* liberal society, creates some
problems. In fact, this approach does not allow us to see some relevant
issues involved in a fair integration of individuals and groups understood
as free and equal participants in a framework constituted by liberal rights
and freedom.

First, given the complexity and the diversification of every liberal
society, it is difficult to identify the *we* in which the ultimate authority
resides. This problem arises especially when it has to be decided whether
a group has to be accommodated and, after it has been accommodated,
what the fairest terms of inclusion should be. Unless one assumes an

[62] Macedo (1998: 79).
[63] Macedo (1998: 73).

unrealistic monolithic image of liberal society, there will be more than one *we* competing for having the last word about such conflict-ridden issues. Moreover, one has to keep in mind that all these opposite *we* will have different interpretations of core liberal principles and, therefore, different and conflicting views about the best answer to diversity. In resolving this conflict, should we apply the majority principle? Sure, it could be applied, but if it is applied without further considerations, there is the risk that the accommodation might become more a matter of power than of justifiable principles. In other words, if the majority decides on the basis of its own principles the groups whose claims are to be accommodated in a liberal society and the ways in which minority groups should transform in order to be included, it would seem, quite contrary to Macedo's intentions, that the hegemony liberalism is assumed to exercise is more than moderate.[64] In this case, one would have a majority imposing its values on minorities asking for accommodation through fair and equitable terms of integration.

Second, it is difficult to imagine that an accommodation process does not produce changes within the majority that receives new (and presumably different) groups. I argue that Macedo's approach is well equipped to see only one side of the coin, that is, the changes required by the minorities. Instead, it is easily predictable that, at least descriptively, the inclusion of new minorities will alter the character of the receiving society. Imagine a homogeneous society that includes minorities having different religious, moral, or political beliefs. Even if we leave aside, for the moment, considerations about the fairness of inclusion, one can claim that the presence of these new minorities will have the effect of creating, in certain senses, a new society.

The process of integration of immigrants shows clearly that the inclusion of new groups involves transformations both in majority and in minorities. In this chapter, I will not take a position in the complex debate between those who argue in favour of open borders and those who oppose it and support restriction to migration.[65] However, for the sake of

---

[64] The hegemony of liberalism is, according to Macedo, *moderate*. See the title of Macedo (1998).

[65] Joseph Carens and Chandran Kukathas can be considered among the best-known supporters of the open border approach to migration, whereas Michael Walzer, David Miller, and Macedo himself are among the theorists arguing for

argument, suppose that the migrants have been lawfully admitted in the new country without posing any serious threat to its economy, stability, and social peace. At this point, following Joseph Carens's description of the method of integration of immigrants, one can envisage a three-stage process.[66] In the first stage, one has the recognition of formal legal equality of immigrants through the grant of legal rights. A liberal state should grant these rights (except political rights) even to individuals who are not yet citizens but reside within its territory. In fact, 'liberal democratic principles may be interpreted in various ways but, however interpreted, they entail a deep commitment to treat those subject to the state authority fairly and equally.'[67] Any liberal state must give reasons in support of differential treatment for citizens and non-citizens. It seems that there is no moral reason for not granting some fundamental legal rights to people who are under state authority although they are not included as full members of the democratic community, in the sense that they are not full citizens.

The second stage of the process of integration of immigrants is the acquisition of citizenship for long-term residents and for their children. It is with the acquisition of citizenship that immigrants achieve that 'status that establishes one's position as a full member of a political community (even though many of the rights of membership cannot be exercised until the children mature)'.[68] In fact, only citizens can participate as equal members in the democratic process of self-determination. At this point, one can wonder whether there could be something beyond legal rights and citizenship, considering that they can coexist with gross inequalities among individual and groups.

According to Carens, there could be a further stage beyond the first two I have briefly discussed here. It is difficult to specify what it would look like in an acontextual way, but one could reasonably expect that there will be 'some sort of mutual adaptation between immigrants and those in the receiving society'.[69] In the chapter on Kymlicka's liberal

---

state control of borders. See Carens (1987, 2005, 2013), Kukathas (2005), Walzer (1983), Miller (2005, 2008, 2016), and Macedo (2007), respectively. For a well-informed discussion, see Pevnick (2011: especially 7–17).

[66] Carens (2005).

[67] Carens (2005: 32–3).

[68] Carens (2005: 36).

[69] Carens (2005: 43).

multiculturalism,[70] the notion of integration of immigrants as a 'two-way street' has been mentioned. It is a process of integration in which both immigrants and the receiving society are reciprocally involved in transformative processes. In that chapter, the comprehensive idea of autonomy used by Kymlicka has been found defective for accounting for what, following Kymlicka himself and Jeff Spinner, has been called 'pluralistic integration'. Now, one could ask if Macedo's theory works better. I already have observed that his politicization of liberalism represents a move towards a more extended philosophical generosity towards diversity. Yet, as the following example will show, his emphasis on the transformative dimension of liberalism is too unilateral, insofar as it allows a grasp over only the transformations demanded from the minorities.

Imagine that a liberal society in which Catholicism is the most common religion receives a significant number of Muslim migrants. Even though the society temporarily rejects full political integration of newcomers, it will be affected by many changes. Let us assume that Muslim children go to public schools with Catholic children. It is easy to foresee that, even without multicultural provisions aimed at accommodating newcomers, classrooms will become at least de facto multicultural.

As David Miller has argued, migrants' contribution to the reshaping of the culture of the nation to which they move is 'a process that happens in any case',[71] even only as a direct consequence of the factual presence of the newcomers. However, relevant normative concerns arise when one considers what the most adequate way of accounting for this process might be. Such an account has to recognize the value of migrants' contribution in a non-residual way insofar as, once they have been lawfully admitted, their status as less than equal citizen is unjustifiable in a liberal perspective.

In fact, later, when the Muslim presence is recognized and accommodated, the changes will be more extended: there will be new study programmes, particular provisions for holidays, and so on. In a subsequent stage, if migrants are fully included in the democratic process and obtain citizenship, one can imagine that 'the acceptance of difference in the public sphere easily leads to a number of changes ... so as to accommodate the newly included groups.'[72] The public space of the receiving

---

[70] See Chapter 2.
[71] Miller (2008: 387).
[72] Galeotti (2002: 200).

society will lodge new individuals with their previously excluded religions, beliefs, moralities, and histories. The earlier Catholic and homogeneous society of our example is not going to exist anymore. It has been replaced by a new society in which both old residents and newcomers have gone through a process of reciprocal transformation.

Once a liberal society, in order to be loyal to its own principles of freedom and equality, decides to accommodate new groups, there are some changes even in the *we* that, according to Macedo, rules on matters of inclusion. In other words, as Bhikhu Parekh has argued in *Rethinking Multiculturalism*, 'We cannot integrate *them* so long as *we* remain *we*.'[73] The process of inclusion of minorities according to fair and equitable terms should be a two-way street, involving transformations both in the receiving society and in the newcomers. Only in that case the conditions for a properly understood *common belonging* hold:

> Immigrants cannot belong to a society unless it is prepared to welcome them, and conversely it cannot make them its own unless they wish to belong to it, with all this entails. Common belonging requires a broad consensus on what is expected of each party, and can only be achieved if each discharges its part of the moral covenant.... Just as immigrants need to commit themselves to the receiving society, it too should make a reciprocal commitment to them.[74]

Thus, a theory such as Macedo's undervalues majority's transformations and, in this way, cannot grasp this other fundamental dimension involved in the accommodation of diversity. This amounts to state that Macedo's understanding of liberalism's transformative practices is incomplete. The stress on the *political* nature of the transformations in which newcomer groups are involved ends up being misleading and too demanding: misleading because, as I tried to show, it blocks us from seeing that majorities transform too; and too demanding because asking minorities to become politically autonomous could be asking for too much.

To be more precise, one could say that Macedo's approach is misleading because it is too demanding. Here, I could, mutatis mutandis, restate the objection I expressed in Chapter 2 against Kymlicka's attempt to liberalize non-liberal minorities (or the criticisms Galston's approach raises

---

[73] Parekh (2006: 204).

[74] Parekh (2008: 87–8).

against Enlightenment liberalism). In the case of Kymlicka, one finds a comprehensive idea of individual autonomy that is ruling the process of accommodation for new groups and individuals. That idea has been found highly tricky. However, even if in a more nuanced form, the same problems appear when the idea of political autonomy is assumed as fundamental. Transforming all individuals into politically autonomous subjects can be tantamount to transforming them into something different from what they are. In addition, this process becomes highly problematic if we consider the fact that it is the majority group which fixes the terms of inclusion according to its own principles and traditions.

The difference concerning the justification of comprehensive and political autonomy is not cancelled. However, even in its political form, autonomy is still too controversial to be the leading value of a liberal theory. This holds especially if, as the previous pages have illustrated, the centrality of autonomy does not allow a complete understanding of the transformative process of individual and group identities involved in accommodating diversity.

In conclusion, autonomy as the main liberal value must be rejected both in its comprehensive and political form. In the next chapter, I will try to present a political form of liberalism that, eschewing any reliance on whatever form of autonomy, aims at being the most adequate theory for dealing with diversity. As it will be clear, it is the rejection of autonomy that allows us to bring to a completion the Rawlsian political turn that, in conjunction with the reliance on the value of autonomy, is unable to give diversity its due.

5

The Liberalism of Diversity

Beyond the Liberal Archipelago

In the previous chapters, I have discussed three liberal approaches to the problem of diversity. Comprehensive forms of liberalism have been rejected in both Will Kymlicka's pro-autonomy and William Galston's pro-toleration version. Kymlicka's liberal multiculturalism has proved to be unable to accommodate diversity. The emphasis on the value of autonomy excessively constrains the accommodation of diversity. The *liberalization* of minorities, considering that they might reasonably reject the primacy of autonomy without posing any threats to the maintenance of a liberal order, does not take their difference seriously. Galston's theory, discarding the view that autonomy is the liberal summum bonum, appears to go one step further. The recognition that there are many legitimate authorities in a liberal society and that liberalism demands respect for 'expressive liberty' would seem a better theory to deal with diversity, at least in *practical* terms. And yet, the notion of value pluralism on which Galston's liberalism relies is not a safe ground: it is a view according to which there are many goods, but Galston seems to translate it in the view that there are many cultures. A similar shift could, contrary to Galston's premises, condone illiberal outcomes and oppression.

The political turn, as Chapter 4 has demonstrated, represents a remarkable theoretical opening to the problem of diversity. The process of politicization renders liberalism independent of comprehensive accounts of good, truth, and religion. In fact, political liberalism, relying on what individuals can share despite their comprehensive loyalties, is more *philosophically* generous than comprehensive liberalism. Political liberalism accepts greater diversity at the foundational level. In the previous chapter, Stephen Macedo's theory has been considered as an example of what I label PA liberalism. The analysis of Macedo's view has shown that his approach aims at accommodating diversity, but is nonetheless rather demanding. In fact, for this liberalism, the acceptance of diversity is subordinate to the *political* transformation of the minorities. The notion of political transformation has been found highly problematic because it prevents us from seeing that the integration of minorities involves reciprocal transformations in both majority and minorities.

The difficulties encountered by the approaches analysed so far prompt me to consider the fourth liberal theory listed in Chapter 1, namely, PT liberalism. The following sections demonstrate that the political turn is brought to completion if it gives up the commitment to autonomy, even to an idea of autonomy understood as a political notion. The requirement of political autonomy of individuals can be too demanding, and, as I observed while examining Macedo's theory, can overlook important dimensions related to the integration of the minorities. Political liberalism, I contend in this chapter, is accomplished and does not betray its philosophical premises when it is coupled with a genuine commitment to toleration. Only in this way is it possible to achieve a theory that combines political liberalism's virtue (its *philosophical* openness towards diversity) with the merits of pro-toleration views (their *practical* receptivity).

If one considers existing liberal literature, Chandran Kukathas's book, *The Liberal Archipelago*,[1] might be seen as representative (in the sense specified in the following pages) of a form of political liberalism according to which toleration, and not autonomy, is the core value. Kukathas's position will be discussed in depth here, and will be used as a significant illustration of the theory I want to argue for. However, notwithstanding its encouraging starting point, Kukathas's theory will be demonstrated to be somehow defective and in need of some substantial adjustments.

---

[1] See Kukathas (2003). If we consider existing literature, Judith Shklar may also be understood as another relevant defender of pro-toleration political liberalism, although her work is less systematic than Kukathas's. John Rawls himself identified Shklar's 'The Liberalism of Fear' as a version of political liberalism. See Rawls (2005) and Shklar (1989). For a discussion of Shklar's liberalism in comparison with Rawlsian political liberalism, see Young (2002: 107–29).

Political pro-toleration liberalism becomes acceptable only when it includes a more substantive idea of unity of the state and the obligations binding individuals to the mainstream society and to the state itself. By 'mainstream society', I mean something like 'political community' or 'political society', namely, the common political space individuals inhabit as individuals and citizens rather than as members of their groups. 'Mainstream society', in this sense, is different from 'state'. The latter is characterized more in an institutional sense, being composed by those institutional mechanisms concerned with policing, law making, war making, and so on.[2]

In this chapter, the next section will explain the sense in which Kukathas's liberalism has to be understood as both political and pro-toleration. In the following section, I will deal with the way in which Kukathas faces the problem of minority rights[3] and their relation with mainstream society. It will be clear that the kind of society Kukathas envisages and recommends is 'an archipelago of different communities operating in a sea of mutual toleration'.[4] These communities are granted an extended degree of autonomy and independence to the point that they can be governed by different and not necessarily liberal principles. Another relevant feature of Kukathas's *liberal archipelago* is that it does not recognize the relevance that has been traditionally ascribed both by liberalism and communitarianism[5] to the existence of a strong mainstream society and to the unity of the state. Further, in Kukathas's thought, freedom of association is fundamental. Individuals are free to join (almost) whichever cultural group, provided that the cultural group respects their right of exit.

In the next section, I will start to consider the limits of Kukathas's model. In particular, I will engage in the critique according to which the liberal archipelago view is descriptively inadequate. I will examine the objection that suggests that this view does not provide an adequate description of liberal democratic societies. It would seem that the liberal archipelago view is unable to account for the life of individuals beyond

---

[2] Kukathas (2003: 209).

[3] For a first-time presentation of Kukathas's view on this, see Kukathas (1995).

[4] Kukathas (2003: 8).

[5] In *The Liberal Archipelago*, Kukathas (2003: 8, footnote 12) admits that his 'sympathies with (some form) of anarchism are quite evident'. See also Kukathas (1996, 2003: Chapter 5).

the group to which they belong. However, as I will show, this critique is not conclusive, and Kukathas has some resources to respond to it. The section that follows will consider the main normative weaknesses of the archipelago view, namely, that it misconceives the relations of individuals with respect to groups, the political community, and the state. In this section, I will enquire into the nature of these obligations and conclude that understanding them as *associative obligations* can render PT liberalism more tenable in comparison with Kukathas's original formulation. Finally, in the last section, I will further amend the liberal archipelago view. Specifically, I will show that a stronger mainstream society is required in order to give efficacy to those exit rights that play such a significant role in Kukathas's liberalism. After that, the necessity of a unitary state will be restated and made explicit in accordance with the basic assumptions of PT liberalism.

A Different Political Liberalism

In 'Two Concepts of Liberalism', Kukathas maintains that 'liberalism is a response to the fact of human diversity, and to the problems it generates.'[6] This answer can be formulated in two different ways. The first considers liberalism as a theory that describes those standards or principles around which a society or community should organize its collective life. From this perspective, '[A] community is a liberal society if its institutions uphold or honour the values which make it liberal.'[7] The values liberalism usually fosters are autonomy (in the Kantian sense) and individuality (in the Millian sense). Furthermore, this version of liberalism assumes that, beyond deep disagreements in many domains, individuals can reach an agreement on some fundamental principles of justice that must rule collective life.

John Rawls's book, *A Theory of Justice*,[8] represents an instance of this way of conceiving liberalism. In his work, Rawls offers

---

[6] Kukathas (2000: 100). In another work, Kukathas (2003: 41) has written: '[T]he human world is marked by diversities—of language, custom, and religion or, more generally, culture. The issue is, how are we to respond to this fact of diversity. What bearing does it have on question of how (and under what institutions) we should live?'

[7] Kukathas (2000: 98).

[8] Rawls (1999a).

a comprehensive justification for a liberal social order, explaining that those who share a recognition of the fundamental importance of certain values would, in a suitably constrained setting, agree to a set of controlling moral principles (justice as fairness), and attendant institutional arrangements (constitutional democracy).[9]

Thus, this model theorizes that people, in appropriate circumstances, agree on some moral principles (which are the basis of a theory of justice) and on certain liberal institutions. However, in disagreement with such an approach, Kukathas argues that 'people may disagree not only about, say, religious matters but also about principles of justice. ... If this is the case, the problem with a solution which recommends agreement to abide by a particular set of rules or principles of justice is that it risks begging the question.'[10] Thus, if one adequately considers the disagreements that characterize modern societies, a convergence on some principles of justice is too difficult to achieve.

Liberalism, according to Kukathas, should not be primarily concerned with principles of justice or with principles that individuals assume as relevant in their private conduct. It should rather be focused on the issue of setting up an umpire who may peacefully resolve disagreements. This way of conceiving liberalism would be, among other things, consistent with liberalism's historical origins and definitional aims. In fact, as Kukathas writes, '[L]iberalism's original concerns were not with justice, or social unity, but with securing a regime of mutual toleration.'[11] It is important to point out that for Kukathas, there is more than one legitimate authority in liberalism, rather than a single umpire who resolves disagreements. Whereas theorists such as Macedo and Galston 'defend liberalism by insisting on the compatibility of respect for diversity and the unity of liberal state',[12] Kukathas does not recognize a particular value in the unity of the state as such.

---

[9] Kukathas (2003: 263).

[10] Kukathas (2000: 101).

[11] Kukathas (2003: 39). Kukathas cites John Locke's *Letter Concerning Toleration* and Pierre Bayle's *Philosophical Commentaries* as 'critical works' in the liberal tradition emerging after European religious wars of the seventeenth century as a theoretical and political attempt to assert the value of liberty of conscience.

[12] Kukathas (2003: 20).

These considerations will be relevant in the following pages, when the metaphor of the liberal archipelago will be explained in detail. Now, it is appropriate to expound the *politicity* and the pro-toleration character of Kukathas's liberalism. He wants to establish liberalism as a *'minimal moral conception'*.[13] Kukathas's liberal theory, like any political theory that wants to be normative, is not devoid of moral content and, for this reason, is a moral conception like any comprehensive liberalism. The difference lies in the fact that whereas comprehensive liberalisms are characterized by substantive commitments, Kukathas's political liberalism looks for the minimal conditions necessary to ensure a peaceful coexistence of different moral positions.

Kukathas is quite explicit in claiming that autonomy is not the main value of liberalism. As Anne Phillips has remarked, '[I]n the political theory literature, the sharpest attack on the idea of autonomy comes in the work of Chandran Kukathas.'[14] In fact, for the author of *The Liberal Archipelago*, an exclusive focus on the idea that autonomy is the centrepiece of human flourishing can prevent individuals to see what really matters, that is, 'being able to live as our conscience dictates'.[15] It should be remarked that, within this conception, a successful life according to the dictates of conscience is not necessarily inspired by the value of autonomy.

The main target of Kukathas's anti-autonomy stance is the idea that revising and examining our ends is a necessary precondition for having a good life: '[T]he critical point here is that unexamined life may well be worth living.'[16] In fact, there could be cases where examining the constitutive features of one's own life can destroy its meaning. Furthermore, there are persons with no interest whatsoever in the assessment, revision, or evaluation of the constitutive features of their personal existence. If this is true, then all those liberal theorists (such as Rawls and Kymlicka), who have claimed that revising the ends of life is a necessary

---

[13] Kukathas (2003: 17). Kukathas admits that his understanding of political liberalism is influenced by Charles Larmore. See Larmore (1996: Chapter 6).

[14] Phillips (2007: 104).

[15] Phillips (2007: 104). The relevance of conscience and of freedom of conscience for Kukathas's liberalism will be discussed in the following pages.

[16] Kukathas (2003: 59).

component of any good human life, have mistakenly assumed as universal a contingent feature of a genuinely successful life. Thus, the claim that public institutions should, more or less directly, promote lifestyles that recognize the universal meaning of the examined life comes to be an undue imposition of a truth assumed as generally accepted despite the disagreement around it.

Kukathas, on the contrary, argues that 'a society or community is a liberal one if, or to the extent that, it is tolerant.'[17] In Kukathas's view, toleration is not that demanding a virtue. It does not require that the object or subject of toleration be respected or admired. In fact, 'toleration requires little more than indifference to those who are, or that which is, tolerated.'[18] This account of toleration is starkly different from other popular and influential liberal accounts. Political theorists such as Deborah Fitzmaurice, Kymlicka, and Rawls,[19] notwithstanding crucial differences among their views, all defend the value of toleration in an indirect way. They share a commitment to autonomy, and it is this very commitment that defines the boundaries of what must be tolerated. In other words, all these approaches 'presuppose the existence of a liberal order: that is, an order in which the value of autonomy, embodied in principles of justice, is authoritatively upheld in public sphere'.[20] Thus, there is a common moral standpoint that establishes the practices that must be tolerated and those that must be coercively discouraged. This means that, in this conception, toleration can only be extended to those practices that respect the core value of the liberal order, which is autonomy.

It is quite common that liberal theories relying on a pro-autonomy view of toleration tend to have a 'liberalizing impulse'.[21] This impulse might authorize objectionable interventions aimed at the transformation of minorities into something that minorities themselves could despise or reject due to the fact that the values imposed from outside might be completely different from their own values and cultural practices.[22] At the foundation of the pro-autonomy concept of toleration lies the idea

---

[17] Kukathas (2003: 23).

[18] Kukathas (2003: 23).

[19] See Fitzmaurice (1993), Kymlicka (1995), and Rawls (1999a).

[20] Kukathas (2003: 125).

[21] Murphy (2012: 67).

[22] See Chapter 2.

that 'when groups cease to respect the freedom or autonomy of individuals in their midst, toleration is no longer warranted.'[23] Kukathas rejects this view for two main reasons. First, it assumes, without proper justification, that in a liberal society there is an established moral order that can set the boundary condition of toleration, which is of what should or should not be tolerated. Second, such an approach is concerned more with the perpetuation of liberal order than with the respect for dissenters, and, as Kukathas argues, this can create risks of 'intolerance and moral dogmatism'.[24]

The aforementioned reasons are enough, in Kukathas's view, to set aside the pro-autonomy conception of toleration in favour of an alternative view. In particular, he wishes to defend a conception that grants an independent value to toleration. In this perspective, toleration does count, in part, 'because it checks or counters moral certitude':[25] people are fallible and so, tolerating different and dissenting beliefs can be an answer to the awareness of the limits of human ability to know. However, these considerations do not seem to go beyond an instrumental defence of toleration. If we stop here, toleration is to be considered valuable since it allows the prevalence of true beliefs over false ones, namely, it is an instrument for the attainment of truth. Going beyond instrumental arguments for toleration, Kukathas adds that toleration 'is also valuable because it is the condition which gives judgments worth'.[26] Here, Kukathas relies on the Kantian argument that specifies that reason depends upon a public realm of freedom. A full exposition of this argument is well beyond the scope of this chapter, but it would suffice to say that reason becomes authoritative only in a public arena in which it is continuously subject to criticism and scrutiny and in which different positions and viewpoints are tolerated. Thus, in order to avoid compromising the authority of reason, 'toleration is vitally important'.[27]

Up till now, I have shown the way in which Kukathas's liberalism can be understood as both political (for what concerns the justification) and

---

[23] Kukathas (2006: 110).

[24] Kukathas (2003: 126).

[25] Kukathas (2003: 126).

[26] Kukathas (2003: 126).

[27] Kukathas (2003: 127). To explain Kant's position about the public use of reason, Kukathas quotes Kant (1970) and O'Neill (1989).

pro-toleration (for what concerns the core value). Thus, it can be argued that according to the taxonomy I have elaborated in the first chapter of this book, Kukathas's theory is an illustration of PT liberalism. In the next section, I will discuss the model of society endorsed by Kukathas and the way he thinks diversity should be dealt with.

The Archipelago Society and the Politics of Indifference

In *The Liberal Archipelago*, Kukathas argues that 'the free society described by liberalism is not a stable social unity created or upheld by a shared doctrine. It is rather a collection of communities associated under laws which recognizes the freedom of individuals to associate as, and with whom, they wish.'[28] Thus, the archipelago society is composed of many communities, which, like islands composing an archipelago, float in a sea of reciprocal toleration. Individuals are free to join groups of whatever character, even illiberal ones. Nevertheless, it is important to observe that membership in a group is not exclusive. An individual, in fact, can join different groups, and these groups can contribute to the shaping of her/his life in different ways.

In Kukathas's model, the role of the state is sensibly less extended than the one recognized by other liberal writers. For instance, Kukathas sees as opponents of his liberal archipelago all those liberal theories that deem it a duty of the state to uphold and promote justice, or better, liberal justice. In fact, considering that the justice these states aim at enhancing is a liberal conception of justice, they assume that their main task consists in liberalizing society and groups. However, according to Kukathas, neither the liberalization of society nor the liberalization of groups should be among the legitimate aims of a state. As argued earlier, the state should not be concerned with the advancement of a conception of justice, but should only care about the preservation of order in a context in which different groups can enter into conflict.[29]

---

[28] Kukathas (2003: 19).

[29] Bhikhu Parekh (2006: 119) considers Kukathas as expressing a *proceduralist view* of political integration: '[I]n the proceduralist view the deep moral and cultural differences to be found in multicultural societies cannot be rationally resolved, and our sole concern should be to ensure peace and stability.' Later, Parekh (2006: 119) adds: '[A]ccording to the proceduralist the formal and minimal

Thus, the state should work as an umpire, with no specific aims apart from the achievement of peaceful and ordered coexistence of potentially conflictual individuals and groups.

Kukathas specifies that the state 'is only *an* umpire—not *the* umpire',[30] but it is still an important one due to the nature and the dimension of its coercive power. Overall, the attitude of Kukathas towards the state is replete with 'scepticism and suspicion'.[31] The existence of a strong central state represents a menace to individual liberty as long as the conformity to a centralized administrative apparatus can generate significant suppressions of individuals' freedom to live as their consciences suggest. The anxiety for social and political unity, Kukathas contends, has always been extremely dangerous for social peace, especially for those societies marked by irreducible deep disagreements. History is full of examples of the state being 'the most powerful instrument of oppression and domination we have known'.[32] The religious persecutions in Europe of the sixteenth century, although apparently based on religious and theological reasons, were determined by the necessities of the rising nation-states: '[R]uling authorities were interested ... in the problem of establishing and securing the borders of the emerging state, and settling the issue of the position of the church within it. To put it in another way, they were interested in the problem of national unity.'[33] Contemporary states face completely different historical circumstances, but still, according to Kukathas, a quest for unity poses a persistent threat to toleration and acceptance of diversity.

After having explained the liberal archipelago metaphor and sketched the function that a state should have in Kukathas's theory, I proceed to analyse how the problem of diversity is dealt within this version of PT liberalism. The starting point for this analysis is a passage from the first chapter of *The Liberal Archipelago*, in which Kukathas, arguing against

---

state combines maximum political unity with maximum diversity; the former because it stays clear of its citizens' moral and cultural disagreements and makes no controversial demands on them, the latter because it imposes the fewest constraints on their choices.'

[30] Kukathas (2003: 213).
[31] Murphy (2012: 68).
[32] Kukathas (2003: 159).
[33] Kukathas (1999: 69).

Galston[34] and other pro-diversity liberals, writes: '[D]iversity is not the value liberalism pursues but the source of the problem to which it offers a solution.'[35] It is simply a fact of social life that there is a plurality of cultures, religions, and languages. Liberalism takes the wrong direction if it aims at protecting or celebrating this diversity. Kukathas argues that diversity has no intrinsic value, in the sense that it is not valuable as such. Rather, it is easy to observe that 'in some contexts, uniformity is preferable'.[36] Consider, for example, the degree of homogeneity required in a church or in some kind of political associations.

At this point, one could ask: what should be the right liberal attitude towards diversity? Should liberal states recognize the diversity of groups, communities, and associations?[37] What is the right course of action for a liberalism that wants to accommodate the demands of recognition advanced by groups? Kukathas's answer is very simple. He claims that 'liberalism is indifferent to the groups of which individuals may be members, it recognizes the freedom of individuals to join or form groups or to continue to belong to groups into which they may have been born—but it takes no interest in the interests or attachments which people might have.'[38] Thus, given that the only interest of the liberal state resides in the preservation of an ordered peace in which individuals and groups must be free to pursue their own ends, any state action involving some form of recognition for groups has to be considered illegitimate. This holds both

---

[34] For considerations related to this point, see the section, 'Sources of Liberal Theory and Galston's Liberal Pluralism', in Chapter 3.

[35] Kukathas (2003: 29).

[36] Kukathas (2003: 32). Similar doubts about the intrinsic value of diversity have been raised by Daniel Weinstock. He argues against those who consider diversity as a universal value, that is, the more the diversity, the more 'the human world will be richer in value'. Weinstock asks, 'richer for whom?', and claims that diversity is 'only good to realize values if human beings can in some way or other benefit from them'. See Weinstock (1997: 493).

[37] Liberal theorists have often been criticized for being inhospitable to difference. In particular, liberals have been criticized since their aspirations to universality reflect the standards of the dominant culture and disrespect the identities of minorities that demand some form of recognition; see Taylor (1992). Kukathas (1998) deals with these objections.

[38] Kukathas (1997b: 135). For similar considerations, see Kukathas (1998: 691).

when the recognition remains within the liberal domain (consider, for instance. Kymlicka's liberal multiculturalism) and when it goes beyond liberalism (for instance, when recognition rests on an objection to liberalism's incapacity to accommodate diversity).[39]

The reasons for denying the desirability of the politics of recognition (through differentiated rights and policies) are related to the alleged 'pernicious consequences'[40] of recognition itself. As it has been observed beforehand, groups are not natural entities. They are 'mutable social formations that change size, shape, and character as society and circumstances vary'.[41] Thus, whenever a state *creates* a group through political recognition, in addition to some epistemological obstacles,[42] the state could be creating the conditions in which people find incentive to identify with the group at the same time. For instance, when a state recognizes a certain category of persons as particularly disadvantaged, people could aim at belonging to this group in order to receive the benefits associated with identification with such a group.[43]

However, regardless of consideration on the stability and composition of groups, the main problem consists in the fact that 'recognition is troubling because it signals an elevation of the conflict between groups over material gains into conflicts over the identity of the society.'[44] The first kind of conflict can be worrisome, but, being concerned with mundane interests, it can be resolved through compromise. The second kind of conflict, since it involves 'ethereal identities', is less open to compromise and, for this reason, far more dangerous.[45] Additionally, assuming recognition to be a universal ambition of groups is an extremely contentious aim for public policies. In fact, not all groups aim at being recognized. For instance, some religious conservative communities such as the Amish or the Hutterites do not want to be recognized. They wish to be left alone

[39] For theories arguing that recognition entails going beyond liberalism, see Crowder (2013: Chapter 5).

[40] Festenstein (2000: 74).

[41] Kukathas (1998: 693).

[42] How should the boundaries be fixed between those who belong to the group and the outsiders? Are there criteria beyond any reasonable doubt?

[43] Kukathas (1998: 693).

[44] Kukathas (1998: 693).

[45] Joppke (2010: 100).

and want to live their life in (almost) complete isolation from the rest of the society.

In Kukathas's liberalism, the scepticism towards recognition goes hand in hand with the acknowledgement of great significance to freedom of association. Individuals are free to join whatever groups or community they like. For him, freedom of association is so broad that it also allows individuals to join even illiberal communities. In fact, according to Kukathas, a liberal society is not necessarily composed of liberal communities.[46] As argued earlier, for him, liberalism is not a theory of justice but a theory aiming at the peaceful coexistence of different and potentially conflicting communities. Thus, an illiberal group can be tolerated as long as it does not pose a risk to the security of the society as a whole, and does not impose its authority on people who want to exit its domain. In fact, freedom of association is not without limits. In Kukathas's theory, individuals are free to associate, but they must also enjoy 'a substantive freedom to exit',[47] in the sense that they should be really free to leave their community and join others. It is fair to claim that, for Kukathas, the right of exit should be understood as nothing more than a right to repudiate authority. A community can exercise authority over its members only when they acquiesce.[48]

However, freedom of exit, as it may be important, is not an ultimate value. In fact, it is based on freedom of conscience. For Kukathas, the latter 'is the basis for a very important freedom: to dissociate from people or communities or traditions or standards one cannot abide'.[49] Thus, when we respect someone's freedom to leave her/his group, we are actually respecting her/his conscience. However, what exactly is conscience? As we know from Kukathas's complex account of human interests, it is a moral sense that directs individuals' lives. The interest in living according to the requirements of conscience, that is, having a free conscience, is considered a fundamental human interest upon which there is an almost universal convergence:

[46] Kukathas (1995: 249).

[47] Kukathas (1995: 252).

[48] For Kukathas, acquiescence is the basis of political obligation. In fact, he maintains that 'the basis of any association's or community's authority is not any right of the group to perpetuation, or even existence, but the acquiescence of its members' (Kukathas [2003: 96]).

[49] Kukathas (2006: 115).

... the remote Aborigines of Australia; the fifteenth-century samurai; the Ibo tribesman; the Irish Catholic living in twentieth-century Dublin; the Hasidic Jew in New York; and the Branch Davidian in Texas. While these peoples differ substantially in their understandings of what is right (although there may also be a substantial overlapping of values shared) ... they all share an interest in being able to follow their consciences.[50]

Freedom of conscience is understandable as 'inner freedom', but in a minimal sense. It captures three important ideas: first, it accounts for the fact that individuals have the capacity to distinguish what is right from what is wrong, and that they should not be coerced to act in ways they consider wrong. Second, 'freedom of conscience recognizes that people's ideas of right and wrong differ.'[51] Third, freedom of conscience accommodates the old liberal conviction that authentic beliefs on how to behave and on what to believe should not be imposed. From these remarks, one can realize that, for Kukathas, freedom of conscience is neither autonomy nor self-direction. In fact, even non-autonomous persons can have free conscience (understood in the way just sketched) provided they are not required to conform to what they do not endorse.

Freedom of conscience plays a significant role in the liberalism of Kukathas. In the sociopolitical domain, the relevance of freedom of conscience is not limited to grounding the right of exit. Freedom of conscience also explains the fact that the liberal archipelago can lodge illiberal groups and authorities. This can be explained through two reasons. First, people can reject the value of having a free conscience and can decide to submit themselves to the will of an authoritarian leader. Second, the conscience of dissenters is not the only conscience that should be recognized as valuable. As Matthew Festenstein remarks, '[T]he majority can have a conscientious commitment to suppress dissent, and to preserve the religious, ideological or cultural integrity of the group.'[52] Thus, also the conscience of those who wish to suppress dissent should be taken into consideration. Nonetheless, Kukathas contends that this does not pose a huge problem for dissenters since, as we already know, they are free to leave their group. However, is this sufficient guarantee for the protection of the rights of dissenters? Among other issues, the following

---

[50] Kukathas (2003: 55).
[51] Kukathas (2006: 115).
[52] Festenstein (2005: 94–5).

sections deal with these concerns, and also provide a general evaluation of Kukathas's approach.

The Archipelago View of Society and Its Limits

As the discourse in the previous pages informs us, the good society envisioned by Kukathas is a collection of different groups with few (if any) relationships. The groups, seen as the islands of a tolerant archipelago, enjoy an extended degree of independence provided that they leave individuals free to dissociate and do not threaten the peace and stability of other groups. As George Crowder has written, '[T]he good society [for Kukathas] is one in which groups simply leave one another alone.'[53] This theory has stimulated a lively debate, bred controversies, and been criticized at length. Many theorists have posed objections to its normative assumptions, and to the fact that it misrepresents the character of liberal societies. In other words, critique has been focused on both its descriptive and normative dimensions. In this section, I will account for some of the objections to the descriptive weaknesses of the liberalism endorsed by Kukathas. The following sections will deal with the normative objections.

In 'Liberalism, Multiculturalism, and the Problem of Internal Minorities',[54] Daniel Weinstock claims that the archipelago view of society is a sociological assumption shared by many theorists who discuss the problem of minority rights. In fact, although Kukathas is the one who defends such a view in a radical form, there are some other contemporary writers such as John Gray, Joseph Raz, and Jeff Spinner-Halev[55] who, to a certain extent, share a similar view. All these scholars see 'political society ... as formed by discrete, insular communities that happen to share space, and that willy-nilly must come to an understanding of how to govern the commons'.[56] This view grants maximum autonomy and authority to groups to the detriment of the central state's prerogatives.

Weinstock aims at contesting the two assumptions at the basis of the archipelago view of society: the *independence* assumption; and the *completeness* assumption. According to the independence assumption, the

---

[53] Crowder (2013: 54).
[54] Weinstock (2007).
[55] See Gray (2000b), Raz (1994), and Spinner-Halev (2001).
[56] Weinstock (2007: 257).

processes through which individuals shape their identity take place exclusively within the groups to which an individual belongs. This process of identity formation is independent of what happens outside the group, namely, in the rest of the political society. The completeness assumption claims that the bond between individuals and groups is so tight that the group completely accounts for the identity of its members. Weinstock argues that once we accept these assumptions, 'people are thought of as relating to the public sphere and to other communities exclusively as members of a particular community (the completeness assumption), and as forming their identities within those communities (the independence assumption).'[57] The problem for the archipelago view, Weinstock contends, is that both assumptions are implausible.

The independence assumption mistakenly takes for granted the insularity and the isolations of groups, whereas it is a fact that groups and their cultures interact and dialectically evolve. With the exception of a few conservative religious groups such as the Amish and the Hutterites, groups in a liberal society cannot be depicted in the way required by the independence assumption. In fact, 'orthodoxy and insularity are not the natural states of cultures.'[58] The completeness assumption is flawed as well. It does not recognize that 'typically, individuals belong to a plurality of groups'[59] (such as churches, political parties, and professional or recreational associations), none of which can completely account for the character of a person. Both the independence and the completeness assumptions take exceptional and extreme cases as paradigmatic of the social life in contemporary liberal societies. It would seem that once we accept such views, partial citizens[60]—namely, those people who live in insular communities, ignore the demands of liberal citizenship, and make no substantive claims on the whole society—are the norm rather than the exception in a contemporary liberal society.

In summary, Weinstock concludes that the archipelago view is descriptively inadequate.[61] To be fair, this objection is slightly

[57] Weinstock (2007: 258).

[58] Weinstock (2007: 262).

[59] Weinstock (2007: 262).

[60] Spinner-Halev (1999: 71).

[61] Spinner-Halev advances a similar argument. He suggests that 'Kukathas' vision of society is odd, and it does not reflect how liberal societies work in practice' (Spinner-Halev [2000: 83]).

exaggerated. Although it has an element of truth, Kukathas's theory does have resources to defend itself from this line of criticism. In fact, in *The Liberal Archipelago*, he argues that 'groups are themselves not in any way natural or fixed entities but mutable social formations which change shape, size, and character as society and circumstances vary.'[62] So, it is difficult to conclude that, for him, the insularity of some small conservative groups is the normal condition of groups within the wider societies in which they live. Additionally, as far as the completeness assumption is concerned, Kukathas is very clear in stating that 'few, if any, communities can constitute an individual's identity because few, if any, individuals are locked in a single community which leaves no room for other attachments to which the group is indifferent. In this sense, (almost) all communities are partial communities.'[63] Thus, in general, communities are not all-encompassing as Weinstock's objections would drive us to believe.

A full acknowledgement of the fact that cultural communities do not live in isolation from the rest of the society can be found in 'Are There Any Cultural Rights?', which is the first seminal statement of Kukathas's liberalism. In the essay, he argues that although each group should have the right to govern its collective existence according to its principles, 'no community within a wider society can remain entirely untouched by the political institutions and the legal and moral norms of the whole.'[64] It is enough to consider how exit rights, which are fundamental to Kukathas's approach, transform the nature of particular communities. When an individual is free to leave, the structure of her/his community is inevitably transformed, 'particularly if the formal right comes with substantive opportunities'.[65] For instance, in a hierarchical and patriarchal community that recognizes the right of exit, it would be unimaginable that the relations between men and women would remain the same as in the absence of the right. As a matter of fact, the structure of a group changes when the weak can leave, or can threaten to leave, the group. It is possible that, due to the possibility of losing members, the most powerful do not oppress the weak as much. Alternatively, it can happen that the weak just go away, again changing the composition of the group. In both cases, the

---

[62] Kukathas (2003: 251).
[63] Kukathas (2003: 171).
[64] Kukathas (1995: 249).
[65] Kukathas (1995: 249).

group is different from what it was before the existence of the right of exit.

Thus, at the conclusion of this section I claim that, despite its plausibility at first glance, the objection concerning the description of the social reality does not present a lethal blow to the archipelago view. The main problem with this view, as will become clear in the following section, is that it misrepresents the actual relations of individuals with groups, mainstream society, and the state. Kukathas visualizes the existence of some sort of relations and obligations owed by individuals to groups, mainstream society, and state. Nevertheless, the obligations recognized by Kukathas are too weak to guarantee an adequate common space among groups and to ground an idea of state as substantive as the principles of PT liberalism themselves would require.

Varieties of Obligations in the Archipelago Society

This section will present some thoughts on the normative inadequacy of the archipelago view. Here I will use, again, Weinstock's views as the starting point of the analysis. He argues that even groups thought to be insular have relations with the mainstream society and may receive benefits from it: '[T]heir proximity and participation in society means that they are not to be thought of solely as formulating claims against the state and the broader society within which they live. They must also be thought of as having obligations toward the state and the broader society.'[66] Put differently, all the groups receive some benefits from the mainstream society, and those benefits ground obligations for those particular groups towards the rest of the society. Consistent to the archipelago image, Weinstock writes that 'since citizens of modern societies actually spend quite a bit of time in the waters separating groups from one another, they all have a responsibility to make sure that they are suitable to the needs of all.'[67] Thus, apart from rare cases of complete isolation, even members of conservative and remote communities must be considered citizens of the mainstream society quite independent of

[66] Weinstock (2007: 261).

[67] Weinstock (2007: 261). Weinstock easily switches from group to individual obligations. Hereafter, I will only consider individual's obligations.

their likes. Thus, they have obligations that bind them to the social world outside their group.

These remarks establish that groups and mainstream society interact in various ways. These interactions entail some obligations, and the archipelago model needs to be amended with the addition of an idea of mainstream society that is more substantive than the one envisioned in *The Liberal Archipelago*. Kukathas, as I argued earlier, does not dismiss the existence of relations between groups and mainstream society. He also presents some thoughts regarding the obligations that hold between groups and the political community (what we call 'mainstream society'). The latter is nothing more than another 'partial association' in the same way as other groups. Without doubt, the obligations groups owe to the political community are significant for people because the political community, through the coercive apparatus of the state, can affect their lives in various ways. Nonetheless, Kukathas argues, people are attached more to their group than to the political community:

> The obligations they owe the political community are ... relatively weak, since they do not spring from any deep commitment to the other members which is thought (mistakenly) to be a necessary feature of this form of association. The obligations individuals owe may, in some circumstances, be indirect inasmuch as they emerge not out of an immediate claim the political community has upon the individual but out of the fact that other communities to which the individual belongs are party to the convention or settlement which creates or sustains the political society. Political obligation stems from our acquiescence in the authority of those associations which have themselves accepted the authority of the state.[68]

Thus, the relation between individuals and the political community is generally indirect. Individuals primarily belong to their communities and, as acquiescing members of those communities, are part of the political community, although only in a feeble and derivative way. This statement is problematic for at least two reasons. First, it seems to relapse into the 'independence assumption', in the sense that the process of identity formation seems to be completely internal to the group. Second, this way of conceptualizing political obligations, that is, considering individuals mainly as members of groups, hardly ensures that people might care

[68] Kukathas (2003: 209).

in a proper way for 'the waters separating groups from one another'.[69] The lives of individuals seem to be almost completely absorbed by their respective communities and, hereupon, there is no place for collective efforts aimed at caring for the common space people inhabit as individuals. If, as demonstrated in the previous section, there are good reasons for rejecting both the independence and the completeness assumptions, individuals should be seen as living in the common waters qua individuals, not as members of a group. Thus, another account of political obligations, though consistent with PT liberalism, is required. It has to be different from the one grounded in the acquiescence of individuals to the authority of their group and should focus more on individuals. In this sense, political obligations should be more of an individual than a group-based concern.

The fair play approach to political obligation is an obvious candidate to be considered here. After all, Weinstock's observations at the beginning of this section clearly seem to be a reformulation of the principle of fair play as the source of political obligation. The idea behind this approach is that when people participate in a cooperative enterprise, and when this cooperation is both decently fair and produces benefits, everyone is obliged to bear a fair share of the burdens generated by the beneficial practice.[70] Rawls has masterfully defined the fair play theory of political obligation in this passage worthy to be quoted at length:

> Suppose there is a mutually beneficial and *just scheme of social cooperation*, and that the advantages it yields can only be obtained if everyone, or nearly everyone, cooperates. Suppose further that cooperation requires a certain sacrifice from each person, or at least involves a certain restriction of his liberty. Suppose finally that the *benefits produced by cooperation* are, up to a certain point, free: that is, the scheme of cooperation is unstable in the sense that if any one person knows that all (or nearly all) of the others will continue to do their part, he will still be able to share a gain from the scheme even if he does not do his part. Under these conditions a person who has accepted the benefits of the scheme is bound by a duty of fair play to do his part and not to take advantage of the free benefits by not cooperating.[71]

[69] Weinstock (2007: 261).

[70] The classical formulation of the principle of fair play can be found in Hart (1955).

[71] Rawls (1999b: 122); emphasis added.

Thus, for fair play theorists, society has to be understood as a just scheme of cooperation that produces benefits for people who take part in this joint activity. The beneficial nature of social cooperation, and mainly the binding nature of these advantages, has generated a huge debate. For instance, Robert Nozick has denied that someone is bound to cooperate after he has received some benefits as an outcome of a cooperative enterprise.[72] From a completely different perspective, theorists such as George Klosko have argued that societies conceived as cooperative enterprises 'provide public goods that are indispensable to the welfare of the community. In these cases the indispensability of the goods overrides the outsider's usual right to choose if he wishes to cooperate.'[73] However, in the following section, I will not handle the idea that suggests that social cooperation provides benefits to people and that these benefits create obligations on those who receive them. My view is that questioning the assumption of society as a fair and equitable scheme of social cooperation suffices to show that the fair play approach is not a viable option when one has to account for the obligations in a way consistent with PT liberalism.

In general, fair play theories strongly rely on the assumption that in order to generate binding political obligations, a society has to be just and has to represent a fair scheme of cooperation. In other words, there is a robust conceptual link between the justice of the cooperation and the creation of binding commitments. As John Simmons has argued, '[O]nly when the scheme or institution in question is just can any obligations of fair play arise.'[74] Thus, fair play theorists presuppose that genuine obligations are created only when the society can be understood as a just cooperative scheme.

The problem with this assumption is that one cannot accept, without further argument, that social cooperation takes place according to norms of justice. That social cooperation is just can be at the most a desideratum, but it is far from being a description of actual societies. The troubles for supporters of the fair play theories increase if one considers that the requirement that a society be just in order to generate binding commitments in its citizens risks to be too indeterminate and demanding. What

---

[72] Nozick (1974, especially Chapter 5).

[73] Klosko (1987). For a more recent and systematic defence of the principle of fair play, see Klosko (2004).

[74] Simmons (1979: 312).

level of justice in a society obligates its citizens to be somehow loyal? Also, what would happen if a society were not perfectly just? Would it be able to regulate the conduct of its citizens? The replies of fair play theorists are not always as convincing as one would wish them to be. However, even in the presence of convincing answers, a crucial difficulty still remains.

In fact, the main weakness of this approach lies in its inconsistency with a realistic account of the political life of a society in which pluralism and difference are the norm rather than the exception. As John Horton argues, 'so much of politics is about coercion and the threat of coercion, about managing fundamental conflicts of value and interest', that the image of society offered by the supporters of fair play risks to be 'overly comfortable and optimistic'.[75] Thus, assuming that society works according to a concordance of interests might obscure that widespread disagreement is a permanent condition of pluralistic liberal democratic societies. The harmony of interests underlying the fair play theories is not a reasonable expectation from societies aiming to give diversity its due, especially those governed by the principles of PT liberalism. In such societies, people tend to disagree on many things, and justice is something on which people hardly will find an agreement. Further, as argued earlier in the section, 'A Different Political Liberalism', justice is not within PT liberalism's domain of concern. Thus, the justification of political obligation cannot be grounded on it. In fact, grounding political obligation on justice would amount to deny the possibility of having political obligation at all.

PT Liberalism and Associative Obligations

The previous section concludes that fair play theories, contrary to Weinstock's suggestions, cannot provide a solid support to political obligations within PT liberalism. In this section, I will argue that understanding political obligations as associative obligations, in the sense that is specified later, is a rather more promising theoretical enterprise. However, I do not aim at providing a full philosophical justification of political obligations as associative obligations. I want to show that, although not in consonance with Kukathas's understanding on political obligations, this approach to political obligations can make adequate

---

[75] Horton (2010: 91).

sense of the relations of individuals with groups, mainstream society (or political community),[76] and state within the framework of PT liberalism.

Ronald Dworkin's work is the standard point of reference for those who conceive of political obligations as associative obligations. In *Law's Empire*, he has written that associative obligations are 'the special responsibilities social practices attaches to membership in some biological or social group, like the responsibilities of family or friends or neighbours'.[77] According to this account, people have associative obligations in virtue of the membership of some group. The basis of these obligations is the relation such membership creates between us and the others. As Margaret Gilbert has argued, membership can 'in and in itself involve obligations'.[78] This means, among other things, that obligations do not emerge only out of a voluntary act.

Antivoluntarism[79] is, in fact, one of the main features of the associative account of political obligations. Political societies, for the advocates of the associative view, are far from voluntary associations. We do not choose societies where we are born. This amounts to saying that belonging does not emerge out of a voluntary commitment. Antivoluntarists argue that 'insofar as membership in political societies clearly carries with it certain duties or obligations, the nonvoluntary character of membership entails that our political obligations also fall on us independently of our voluntary choices.'[80] According to Simmons, in addition to antivoluntarism, this view of political obligations is marked by four more features. First, an associative account of political obligations recognizes the 'authority of shared moral experience', in the sense that it aims at being realistic and at accounting for how people perceive obligations in their ordinary lives. Second, political obligations are particular obligations. In fact, we feel that they are owed not to a generic social group but just to *our own* society. Third, families are a paradigmatic example of a social environment in

---

[76] Here, only those obligations are considered that individuals owe to their group and to the mainstream society. Obligations of a group to the society will not be discussed.

[77] Dworkin (1986: 196). For a more recent discussion, see Dworkin (2011: Chapter 14).

[78] Gilbert (2006: 18).

[79] Simmons (2001: 66).

[80] Simmons (2001: 67).

which associative obligations take place: People are born into families independent of their will, and yet feel that they have binding commitments towards their relatives. Finally, political obligations are local. This means that 'local practice can independently generate moral obligations',[81] without any reference to external sources of justification.

In order to evaluate whether an understanding of political obligations as associative obligations is an adequate account for PT liberalism, it is necessary to test the associative account of political obligations in the case of the obligations that individuals have towards their group, their political community, and the state.[82]

The first test, concerning the obligations individuals owe to the group to which they belong, can easily be passed. Groups, especially cultural ones, are collective entities to which people belong without giving their consent. Let us assume that you are born into a community, of course independently of your will. After your birth, you can feel an obligation towards the other members of the group. These obligations are owed just to the members of the group to which you belong, not to a generic ensemble of people with whom you do not have significant relations. You can conceive of these obligations as continuous with the ones you owe to the members of your family. Finally, you can think that the obligations you feel do not require to be justified through external reasons.

Up to this point, it seems that such an account of obligations does not contradict the principles of PT liberalism. We definitely can combine the minimalism and pro-diversity character of PT liberalism with a view of political obligations sketched here. Associative theories fit well with the (sometimes) emphasized role of community within PT liberalism, especially in Kukathas's account. In fact, the associative account of political obligations in general comes up with the acknowledgement of 'the central role that communities, social groups, and family play in shaping our personalities and character' and with the view that 'we cannot conceive of ourselves in isolation from the groups in which we grow up, live, work.'[83]

---

[81] Simmons (2001: 67–70).

[82] Here, one could consider another level of obligations, namely, the obligations one might have towards people belonging to different political societies and states. However, the analysis of these obligations lies beyond the scope of this book.

[83] Van der Vossen (2011: 481).

This means that community plays a constitutive role in the process of definition of our personal identity. Political pro-toleration liberalism can accept this view without particular difficulties. In fact, its tenets admit a pronounced role for communities in the lives of individuals. This role is so broad that the liberal archipelago advocated by Kukathas might accept even massive violations of individual rights and become, according to some critics, a 'mosaic of tyrannies'.[84]

Some problems do appear when one considers the relations between individuals and political community, as also those between individuals and the state. As pointed out earlier, Kukathas has some difficulties in accounting for such relationships and for the obligations that emerge from them. Thus, a better account is needed. A good starting point for my attempt to defend the associative account within the constraints of PT liberalism is represented by Horton's account of political obligations as associative obligations.[85] It is worth remarking that Horton's account concerns the obligations people owe to the *polity*. In what follows, his theory will be exposed and then adapted to my own theoretical aims.

Horton's attempt to show why the polity is a non-voluntary group to which people feel obliged relies on two considerations. First, the polity is valuable for people living under its authority because it ensures peace and social order. However, the value of a polity, Horton argues, is a necessary but not a sufficient condition to explain obligations. In fact, one could acknowledge the value of any polity that grants peace and social order, but a theory of political obligation should explain the special ties linking an individual to *her/his own* polity. Thus, a further consideration is needed, and it concerns the identity-conferring character of the polity. Once a polity has value for its members and once the latter identify with the polity, Horton contends, individuals owe genuine political obligations to the polity.

Let us start with an explanation of why and how the polity has value for those who are ruled by it. Here, I rely on what Horton calls 'the Hobbesian argument'.[86] The idea at the basis of this argument is that if

---

[84] Green (1995: 270). The problems created by an extensive role for groups and the dangers for individuals within them will be briefly dealt with in the next section. These problems are among those that push for an amendment in the liberal archipelago model.

[85] Horton (2010: Chapter 7).

[86] Horton (2010: 176).

human beings aim at living together in groups that are bigger than the ones held together by personal feelings, they need some 'regulatory body'. In fact, even if we do not assume that human beings are necessarily self-ish, plurality itself will create conflicts and contentions. Thus, in order to regulate their disagreements, people need 'an effective coercive authority to provide order, security and some measure of social stability'.[87] If these minimal conditions are not met, the idea of human flourishing (which-ever way you understand it) loses its meaning. In fact, how can someone realize her/his aims and give value to her/his life, if s/he cannot rely on some minimal condition of security and stability?

Note that the Hobbesian argument is less demanding, for instance, than some other idealized views that picture obligations in associative terms. These latter require fraternity as the cement of social relationships and claim that communities have to treat individuals with *equal*[88] concern and respect. For its part, the Hobbesian argument is more parsimonious. It only talks about 'the minimal conditions of order and security'[89] and admits that these baseline conditions can be realized even in non-liberal and non-democratic polities. Thus, conceiving political power as the guarantee of basic order and security, the Hobbesian argument is con-sistent with the main tenets of PT liberalism, as presented in the earlier sections, 'A Different Political Liberalism' and 'The Archipelago Society and the Politics of Indifference'.

As already remarked, the Hobbesian argument should be supple-mented with some further considerations about the special ties between an individual and her/his own polity. In other words, we need a discus-sion on the role membership in a polity plays in the process of citizens' identity construction. A polity, apart from the group to which we belong, represents the ground upon which we conduct our life. It is the context in which we grow up, are educated, and find the cultural options we require in order to shape our lives. It would be difficult to imagine someone completely disencumbered from the polity that has shaped her/his life in multiple ways.

---

[87] Horton (2010: 176).

[88] Dworkin (1986: 200).

[89] Horton (2010: 178). The emphasis on the guarantee of order and peace as the fundamental requirement of political power puts the Hobbesian argument within the camp of the realist political theory. See Galston (2010).

There are two dimensions we have to consider in accounting for political identity: the objective and the subjective. According to the former, the membership of a polity is somehow objective. To be a member of a polity is, in fact, non-voluntary and 'does not depend upon our personal sentiments, emotions, attitudes or points of view: it is concretely manifested in a range of social practices and institutions'.[90] Political identity is real and, since it is connected to the understanding of who we are, has implications from the moral and political points of view. In fact, membership in a certain polity shapes our views in different ways and gives us a vantage point from which we evaluate and judge what is around us. The subjective side of identity, instead, consists in 'an acknowledgment of membership by the member'.[91] This entails that individuals perceive that they are part of the polity and that their flourishing or decaying depends (in part) on the fate of the polity itself. The subjective dimension of political identity, however, is not limited to the acknowledgement that we are collocated in a common historical narrative. In fact, the process of identification with a polity is not completed until people recognize that they share a common political authority. This acknowledgement, Horton observes, is 'the core content of political obligation'.[92]

At this point, after having presented an associative account according to which individuals (directly, not through the groups to which they belong) owe obligations to the polity, we should ask whether this view might be useful for the purposes of the present book. I think one can make sense of it within the scope of this work by arguing that the polity[93] must be seen as including both the state (understood as a set of institutions) and the political society (or the mainstream society, as understood here). Furthermore, one needs to add that the Hobbesian argument relates to the state and to the obligations that individuals owe to the state. Instead, the argument based on identity and membership concerns the mainstream society and the obligations individuals owe to the mainstream society. After all, it is the state with its institutions that guarantees order and security. Then, it is in the political society, understood as the common space shared by people belonging to different groups, that the process of identification takes place.

---

[90] Horton (2010: 183).

[91] Horton (2010: 183).

[92] Horton (2010: 184).

[93] Actually, Horton is not very clear on the meaning of 'polity'.

The Hobbesian argument, in its minimalism, does not present special problems of consistency with PT liberalism tenets. In fact, order, peace, and security are purposes whose relevance for PT liberalism has already been acknowledged in the section, 'A Different Political Liberalism'. Thus, when a state guarantees such goods to people, it is reasonable to expect that these latter owe obligation to the state.

Some issues can emerge from the thoughts on membership and identity related to the mainstream society. However, nothing in this view entails that the process of identity construction exclusively takes place within the mainstream society. The role of the groups to which people belong has already been remarked. Both groups and mainstream society can contribute to shaping the identities of individuals in different forms and without aiming at excluding each other.

The Necessary Mainstream Society and the State

This chapter started with an exposition of some views of Kukathas that challenge the traditional liberal idea of the unity of the state. However, the preceding pages have tried to show that, if correctly understood, the archipelago view of society does not rule out the view that there are connections between individuals, political society, and state. The fluidity of borders among cultural groups is a guarantee that they are not isolated entities, as Kukathas himself is willing to acknowledge. In addition, as the previous section demonstrated, individuals have political obligations towards their political society and to the state, and these obligations can be understood as associative obligations. Thus, notwithstanding the first impression, PT liberalism has to admit the presence of a mainstream society and of the state. In this section, I will analyse another reason in favour of the existence of the mainstream society: the latter is necessary as a guarantee to the effectiveness of the exit rights that, as seen in the section, 'The Archipelago Society and the Politics of Indifference', play a significant role within the overall structure of the liberalism defended here. Further, it will be shown that the presence of a state is required by the same minimal principles upon which PT liberalism relies.

That PT liberalism needs an account of the mainstream society comes from its account of exit rights. In fact, when individuals leave their communities, they should have somewhere to go to, otherwise their exit rights become empty. What happens when dissenters have difficulty in being admitted to another group? Furthermore, the right to be admitted into a new community cannot be implicit in the right of exit. A right such as the right to have a community to join would be too demanding and cannot be clearly specified to the hypothetical receiving communities: Who should receive whom is not plain and, in any case, the integrity of the communities would be violated by such a requirement. Things get further complicated if one considers those people who want to leave their groups and are willing to live as unaffiliated individuals.

A promising solution has been proposed by Jeff Spinner-Halev. He has clearly formulated the thought that a mainstream society is required in order to make exit rights effective. He argues that people who refuse to be part of any group should have the opportunity to access a fairly hospitable mainstream society.[94] For Spinner-Halev, this option is not available in the liberal archipelago view. In fact, if the state is only an umpire (or at best, one of the umpires) among different communities and if it is constituted by groups rather than individuals, it is not well equipped to receive those who do not want to belong to any other group. In this sense, the liberal archipelago would not be a welcoming place for 'unaffiliated individuals'.[95] However, this would be the case despite Kukathas's explicit individualistic premises.[96] These observations are used by Spinner-Halev for arguing against Kukathas. For him, Kukathas's pro-toleration approach 'forgoes tolerance of individuals for tolerance of groups'.[97] Spinner-Halev concludes his critique by suggesting that 'a liberal mainstream society

---

[94] Spinner-Halev (2000: 83).

[95] Spinner-Halev (2000: 83).

[96] In fact, in 'Are There Any Cultural Rights?', Kukathas maintains that individualism—the view that acknowledges 'the moral primacy of the person against the claims of any social collectivity' (Kukathas 1995: 231)—is, in conjunction with universalism and egalitarianism, a core assumption of any liberal argument. In the same essay, the value of groups, cultures, and communities is considered relevant only when they can enhance the well-being of individuals (Kukathas 1995: 233). In *The Liberal Archipelago*, too, Kukathas's individualistic faith is not altered and one can find the statement that the individual is 'the entity with whose good we must ultimately be concerned' (Kukathas 2003: 90) and that the identity of groups is the product of individual interactions.

[97] Spinner-Halev (2000: 84). Brian Barry (2001) has raised similar worries about the possibility that the focus on groups' autonomy can end up in gross oppressions for individuals.

with few requirements for entrance'[98] is the best way to make sure that individuals' exit rights have some effectiveness and, more generally, to rescue the individualistic foundations of liberalism.

I find these views particularly convincing. Political pro-toleration liberalism requires a mainstream society to give a concrete meaning to exit rights. This would fill a gap in the account of PT liberalism that we have considered since the beginning of this chapter. Thus, mainstream society has to find a place within a suitable account of PT liberalism. At this point, one can ask: how should we think about mainstream society in a PT perspective? On this issue, my view departs from Spinner-Halev's solution. He argues that the mainstream society should be defined in pro-autonomy terms. In fact, in *Surviving Diversity*, Spinner-Halev claims that the mainstream society, which he thinks necessary even in order to allow people to live non-autonomous lives, should be a diverse social environment and be supportive of autonomy.[99] Spinner-Halev's liberalism (that cannot be extensively discussed in this chapter) is, at the end of the day, a pro-autonomy liberalism.[100] Thus, notwithstanding a generous attempt to accommodate diversity, his theory is grounded in the value of autonomy and is, therefore, inadequate to address the problem of diversity for the same reasons as presented in Chapters 2 and 4.

The mainstream society required by PT liberalism would be what, following Weinstock's essay, has been labelled as 'common waters'. It should be the common place for individuals coming from different cultural groups. If it is common, as Weinstock puts it, it has to be 'suitable to the ends of all'.[101] If its principles were dependent on the value of autonomy, mainstream society would not achieve this outcome. In other words, autonomy, being itself a contested value, cannot be considered as a default position. Imagine if mainstream society were autonomy driven: it would not be able to accommodate the presence of those individuals who exercise their rights to exit, but do not leave their original community in search of an autonomous (in the sense of rational, self-directed, and

---

[98] Spinner-Halev (2000: 84).

[99] Spinner-Halev (2000: 86).

[100] Spinner-Halev (2000: 86) maintains that 'the primary value of liberalism is autonomy, not citizenship, and people can choose to be bad citizens. Yet the concern for citizenship remains.'

[101] Weinstock (2007: 261).

self-examined) life. In fact, moving out of a community is not tantamount to looking for an autonomous style of human flourishing.

Once we acknowledge that PT liberalism admits the existence of a mainstream society beyond groups and that this mainstream society is not autonomy promoting, it would be fair to inquire how and whether the state fits in this picture, notwithstanding the suspicious attitude towards it, as accounted for in the section, 'The Archipelago Society and the Politics of Indifference'. Remember that the main reason underlying such suspicion is the fear of oppression. As already observed, Kukathas conceives of the state as 'the most powerful instrument of oppression and domination we have known'.[102] In an essay on Brian Barry's *Culture and Equality*,[103] Kukathas cites Australian state intervention to enhance the interests of Aboriginal children as an example of state's oppressiveness: 'assuming that they would be maltreated by their own communities, large numbers of Aboriginal children of mixed descent were, over a period of forty years, removed from their families so that they might be given a good, Christian education.'[104] In this, as in many other cases, the consequences of state action were perilous.

However, Kukathas's normative theory is overawed by history: the fact that the state has (supposedly) been an extraordinary oppressive force does not necessarily mean that it cannot be reformed. Moreover, one should also keep in mind that even smaller communities can be oppressive and that their oppressiveness can be more heinous than state's tyranny. It could be possible and also desirable that if the state is led by the right liberal principles, namely, the ones inspiring PT liberalism, its oppressiveness would disappear to a greater extent. Spinner-Halev seems to take this very route: 'Kukathas worries about the tyranny of the state, but you don't have to eliminate state power to ease this worry; you can, instead, limit its power.'[105] After all, this restriction of power is in accordance both with the precepts of traditional liberalism[106] and with the conception of liberalism outlined in the first chapter of this book.

---

[102] Kukathas (2003: 159).

[103] Barry (2001).

[104] Kukathas (2002a: 198).

[105] Spinner-Halev (2005b: 161).

[106] At least since John Locke and John Stuart Mill, liberalism is concerned with the limits to the state power.

Limiting, though, does not mean eliminating. Far from being something that should be eradicated or loathed for its possible oppressiveness, state power can be seen as somehow necessary[107] to the peaceful perpetuation of a society ruled by PT liberalism.

Craig Carr, more explicitly than Kukathas,[108] argues that, as far as is likely that groups will have many possibilities of interaction and conflict, the maintenance of peace and toleration among them is seriously in danger if we place our trust entirely in the hands of the fate. In fact, for Carr, 'the fact of pluralism necessitates organization, management, and coordination in order to enable groups to live as they wish in the company of others.'[109] That groups conflict among themselves is something that is to be expected. When we acknowledge the fact that individuals and groups do not live in isolation, and especially in modern conditions have frequent occasions to relate, asymmetries of power and other social circumstances can upset social peace and reciprocal toleration. A centralized administrative entity, that is, a state is required to deal with these issues. In particular, the functions of a state in accordance with PT liberalism can be sketched in the following way. First, it has to guarantee that stronger groups do not exploit weaker and poorer ones. In other words, the state should create the conditions for inter-group stability and peace. Second, the state has to work in a manner that the mainstream society is welcoming and responsive to the needs of all.[110] This means that everyone should feel welcome when they leave their original community or, in less dramatic cases, when they spend some time in what we called 'common waters'. Finally, in order not to betray the individualistic premises of liberalism, the state must guarantee fundamental individual rights both within and outside the groups to which people belong.

This account both amends and explicates some aspects of Kukathas's PT liberalism. On the one hand, the discourse on the necessity of a

---

[107] Carr (2010: 92).

[108] 'Unless individuals or groups intend to live in isolation, which in the modern world is not an option readily available, they will have to coexist with others, and find some *modus vivendi*. To the extent that they will have to interact, they will have to abide by mutually accepted laws, and to accept the authority of some third party who will adjudicate disputes.' See Kukathas (2003: 143).

[109] Carr (2010: 90).

[110] After all, the mainstream society does not create by itself the conditions for its own perpetuation.

reasonably strong mainstream society corrects and strengthens the original formulation of PT liberalism. On the other, the arguments on the role of the state both extend Kukathas's ideas and rescue liberalism from anarchical outcomes. In so doing, PT liberalism looks increasingly tenable and capable of accommodating diversity in proper ways. The next chapter deals with the issue of religious pluralism in India and demonstrates how this liberal conception can be effective in a concrete situation.

6

Religious Pluralism and the Role of the State

This chapter is somehow not self-standing, since its main aim is to defend the liberal theory worked out in the previous one against a likely objection someone could raise. Some critics could contend that due to its minimalist character, a liberal state such as the one envisioned by PT liberalism cannot defend an adequate conception of the role of the state in dealing with diversity. It would seem that, in PT liberalism, the state has no consistent role to play and that its functions are rather diminished, as if it were a sort of a *minimal* state such as the one envisioned in the libertarian tradition. According to libertarian thinkers, the state has the monopoly on the legitimate use of the force and is authorized to use it only to defend the rights of the individuals who reside within its borders. For libertarians of this sort, any further action carried out by the state is illegitimate.[1]

In order to prove that PT liberalism is significantly different from libertarianism in the sense just sketched, I will consider the case of India's religious pluralism. In particular, I will criticize some relevant theories about the accommodation of religion pluralism, worked out by Indian theorists relying on some thoughts about the proper extension of the state power that have been worked out in the previous chapter.

Through a discussion on the sound attitude of the state towards religious diversity, I will argue that these theories are too demanding. Due to

---

[1] Nozick (1974).

their grounding in strong and substantive values, the theories I discuss leave too much space for the prerogatives of the state. I will conclude by arguing that PT liberalism has resources to deal with religious diversity even in a complex context such as India, and is preferable to some *local* and influential alternatives theories. Thus, the objection that PT liberalism does not have adequate resources to deal with diversity is misplaced.

In the first section of this chapter, I will briefly present and challenge a particularly widespread view among liberal theorists, namely, the idea that religious issues are not a proper concern of the state. Both Will Kymlicka and Chandran Kukathas, despite the fact that they depart from completely contrasting positions, offer different formulations of the same idea that the state should not be concerned with religious diversity. The former argues that *benign neglect*[2] is the right attitude of the state when religious diversity is at stake, whereas the latter argues in favour of state indifference.[3] However, as the previous chapter has shown, when we account for diversity, the state has a (constrained) role to play. Religious diversity, being one of the manifestations of diversity,[4] should be accommodated by the state in proper ways. Thus, rather than being benignly neglectful or indifferent to religious diversity, the state should accommodate it and restrain its policies according to the principles of PT liberalism.

In the following section, I will consider religious pluralism in India and give an account of some positions that argue for a specifically Indian conception of secularism as a solution to the problems posed by such a huge expression of diversity. As influential examples of advocates of Indian secularism, I will discuss the works of Rajeev Bhargava and Neera Chandhoke.[5] Any attempt to give a general definition of secularism and of the principles on which it relies is rather difficult and, mostly, beyond the aims of the present work.[6] However, for the sake of the argument, one might say that secularism concerns the relations between state and religions, and that the conceptions of secularism that will be exposed in this chapter share the belief that the state acts correctly insofar as it treats equally all the religions professed by its citizens. Other conceptions, such

---

[2] Kymlicka (1995: 107–8).
[3] Kukathas (1998).
[4] Taylor (2011a: 36).
[5] Bhargava (2007) and Chandhoke (1999).
[6] See Maclure and Taylor (2011) and Melidoro (2014).

as the ones denying the equal status of all religious groups, will not be considered because they fall outside the egalitarian concern that is typical of liberalism as here understood.

Then, in the last section, after some remarks about the strongly egalitarian interventions of the Indian state in religious affairs, I will give a critical evaluation of Bhargava's and Chandhoke's works. I will argue that although these theorists have some undeniable merit in their attempt to safeguard the peculiar nature of Indian secularism, they allow excessive state interventions. Particularly objectionable, as it will be argued keeping in mind what PT liberalism countenances concerning the acceptability of state interfering, are those interventions that aim to enforce equality within the internal life of some groups.

Beyond the Benign Neglect and Indifference towards Religion

The idea that a liberal state should not interfere in religious matters is quite widespread among both the advocates and critics of liberalism. The latter see non-interference as the final avowal of the fact that liberalism is nothing more than an anti-religious theory, whose aspiration to universalism and neutrality is insincere, unrealizable, or even hegemonic.[7] The former, who are my focus in this section, argue in different ways that the principles of liberalism themselves end up excluding religion from the domain of state action. Both Kymlicka and Kukathas, advocates of theories I call CA[8] and PT[9] liberalism, respectively, share this view. In the rest of this section, after a brief summary of their accounts on the relation between state and religion, I will argue that both have severe limitations.

Kymlicka maintains that benign neglect is the appropriate attitude of the state when religious diversity is concerned. According to him, a state employs benign neglect when it is limited to ensuring the individual rights of the people but does not interfere in their affairs. For instance, benign neglect with respect to cultural diversity would entail indifference towards the outcomes of the so-called cultural marketplace. When a state is neglectfully benign, it is not interested in the condition of a culture—its flourishing or decaying. It only cares that everyone is free to choose the

---

[7] Chakrabarty (2000) and Parekh (1992).

[8] See Chapter 2.

[9] See Chapter 5.

culture they want to belong to. However, benign neglect, Kymlicka contends, is not a wise policy with regard to cultural diversity. In fact, it would be an appropriate state policy only if a 'strict separation'[10] of state and culture was feasible. In this case, the state could actually be indifferent with regard to how cultural groups live. In fact, the happenings within a society, whether groups flourish or decay, would be outside the domain of state responsibility. Nevertheless, this is not the case, since whenever the state decides, for instance, about an official language for education or when it fixes public holidays, it 'unavoidably promotes certain cultural identities, and thereby disadvantages others'.[11] Whatever the state does, it interferes with the life and conditions of cultural groups. Thus, given the impossibility of a separation, benign neglect does not make much sense where culture is concerned.

Kymlicka claims that these arguments against benign neglect do not apply when religion is at stake. He assumes, in a rather simplistic way and without any argument, that from a theoretical standpoint,[12] state policies with respect to religion can and should be neutral. He argues that a separation of church and state is perfectly achievable, conceivable, and, after all, easy.[13] Thus, for him, while benign neglect does not hold for cultural diversity, it would be perfectly adequate with respect to religious diversity.[14]

However, this conclusion is not acceptable. In the absence of an argument that demonstrates that the separation of religion and state is achievable, benign neglect for religious diversity is as untenable as in the case of cultural pluralism. At its best, as Veit Bader contends, in analogy with cultural diversity, benign neglect in religious matters 'can only result in presumed neutrality hiding actual bias in favour of religious majorities'.[15]

---

[10] Kymlicka (1995: 107).

[11] Kymlicka (1995: 108).

[12] Newman (2003: 271).

[13] Kymlicka (1995: 111). See also Joppke (2010: 24).

[14] More recently, Kymlicka (2009: 2) has acknowledged that a rigid separation of church and state is a myth, since it is quite common that states 'are inevitably involved in the process of recognizing religious groups and of accommodating religious belief'. However, this statement looks more an observation on the always troublesome relation between theory and practice than an acknowledgement of a theoretical weakness.

[15] Bader (2007: 83).

In other words, as it happens when cultural diversity is concerned, a state decides to be benignly neglectful in religious affairs ends up favouring majority religious groups.

Kukathas's position of complete state neutrality in matters of religious diversity is not unexpected. As the previous chapter has demonstrated, for him, indifference is the right liberal attitude when diversity is at stake. Thus, in matters of religious diversity, which is one of the many forms of diversity, the state should refrain from any form of recognition of religious groups, churches, and organizations. Religious groups should be free to compete in the so-called free market of faith, and any outcome that results from such competition has to accepted, provided that all the transactions have not been hindered by an external authority.

At the end of Chapter 5, arguing against Kukathas's liberal model, I listed some reasons why a state, consistent with a proper understanding of the principles of PT liberalism, should be concerned with the management of pluralism, if only to safeguard peace and security (which, to recollect, are at the foundation of PT liberalism itself). We cannot let diversity take its course, especially when majorities and minorities are concerned. In this case, it is easily foreseeable that indifference would end up favouring the stronger groups. These same issues, in absence of a proof that religious diversity is substantially different from diversity in general, hold in the case of religious pluralism. Consider, for instance, a country in which Catholicism is the majority religion. If this country receives a certain number of Muslim migrants and if the political institutions decide to play no role at all in order to be indifferent, it is easy to foresee that Muslim communities will not easily have the conditions they need to thrive and to perpetuate their values and lifestyles. As a matter of fact, the diversity of religious beliefs, belonging, and organization is often characterized by severe differences in terms of numbers and power. Thus, an indifferent attitude would both accentuate these inequalities and render uncertain the conditions for an ordered and peaceful society.

To recall from the previous chapter, PT liberalism accepts state intervention in three cases. First, where both majority and minorities coexist, the state has to guarantee that stronger groups do not exploit weaker and poorer ones. This requires the state to create conditions for inter-group stability and peace. Second, the state should render the mainstream society welcoming and responsive to the needs of all. Thus, the common social space people inhabit as individuals should fairly accommodate all the individuals, irrespective of the community they belong to. Third, consistent with the individualistic foundations of liberalism, the state must ensure that fundamental individual rights are not violated both within and outside the groups to which people belong.

When the state deals with religious diversity, it has to stick to these three rules. In a later section of this chapter, 'Secularism and the Role of the State in Dealing with Diversity', I will discuss the role of the state according to some influential political theories that see secularism as the best answer to the problems posed by religious diversity in India. Before that, both a summary account of religious diversity in India and some relevant theories of Indian secularism will be covered in the next section.

Religious Diversity in India: Secularists' Solution

Diversity is a matter of fact in India. So much so that Bishnu Mohapatra argues it is 'proverbial'.[16] India is home to more than a billion inhabitants who, among themselves, speak about 4,600 languages and dialects. Further, approximately 2,800 ethnic communities and 20,000 caste groups live in the country.[17] If one accounts for the religious divisions in India, one finds that 'India houses all the major religions of the world.'[18] According to the 2011 Census of India, approximately 79.8 per cent of Indians are Hindus, whereas 14.2 per cent are Muslims. Christians, Sikhs, and Buddhists are minority religious groups as they represent 2.3 per cent, 1.7 per cent, and 0.7 per cent of the total population, respectively.[19] Thus, Hinduism is the majority religion in India. To be more precise, Hinduism is the majority religion across all regions with the exception of Manipur, Arunachal Pradesh, Mizoram, Lakshadweep, Nagaland, Meghalaya, Jammu and Kashmir, and Punjab. Muslims are a majority in Lakshadweep and Jammu and Kashmir. Assam, West Bengal, Kerala, Uttar Pradesh, and Bihar also account for a significant percentage of the Muslim population in India.

---

[16] Mohapatra (2010: 221).

[17] Mohapatra (2010: 221).

[18] Mohapatra (2010: 221).

[19] Available at https://www.census2011.co.in/religion.php, accessed 31 October 2019.

The picture of deep diversity[20] in India becomes increasingly complex when one considers that none of the religions present in the country 'is practised in a uniform or undifferentiated way …. Each has witnessed significant reform movements over the centuries; and each has conflicting theological schools and is characterised by internal sectarian differences.'[21] This is true also about the Hindu majority. There is no single mode of being Hindu. There are many Hindu groups and sects (Shaivite, Sanatani, Arya Samaji, Satnami, and so on). Furthermore, the system of belonging to the Hindu religion depends on the caste system as well. In fact, there are Hindus who also a part of various subgroups, such as are Brahmin, Kayastha, Rajput, Jat, and so on.[22]

In other words, fragmentation is a constitutive aspect of Indian religiosity to the extent that one can maintain that India is a 'country of minorities'.[23] Consider furthermore that this diversity is something that India had to face since the beginning of its constitutional history. In fact, contrary to religious diversity in some European countries,[24] in India, diversity did not emerge following a period of alleged religious homogeneity. This equates to say that religious diversity, being somehow inherent to the Indian society, has not worked as a factor that has disrupted established political habits and common traditions.

After this brief account of the religious division in India, one can ask how the state should deal with such a massive and dismaying social phenomenon. Some theorists claim that a peculiar understanding of secularism is the political value needed both to resolve the problems posed by religious diversity and to make possible a peaceful and ordered life in India.

Rajeev Bhargava is among those scholars who, systematically, have tried to argue that an adequate conception of secularism is necessary to ensure a common life despite deep disagreements in matters of ultimate truth.[25] For him, a distinctively Indian secularism is both feasible and desirable.[26] To say that there exists a peculiarly Indian conception of

---

[20] Bajpai (2011: 6–7).
[21] Jayal (2006: 23).
[22] Kishwar (1999: 145–6).
[23] Kishwar (1999: 146).
[24] Citrin and Sides (2008).
[25] Bhargava (1998b: 507).
[26] Bhargava (1998a, 1998b).

secularism amounts to saying that the 'necessary link between secularism and Christianity is exaggerated, if not mistaken'.[27] Further, Bhargava claims that any view according to which requirement of hostility to religion and religiosity as a feature of a secular state is hard to defend. In fact, assuming that secularism, broadly conceived, requires a separation of religion and politics does not necessarily entail the mutual and reciprocal exclusion of the two fields. For Bhargava, different interpretations of the separation of religion and politics are possible. Such a separation can occur at three levels: (*i*) ends; (*ii*) institutions and personnel; and (*iii*) law and public policy.[28] When religious and political powers are connected at levels (*i*), (*ii*), and (*iii*), there is a theocracy. In theocracies, there is no distinction between mundane (that is, state) and sacred (that is, religious) ends. Furthermore, the same persons exercise both spiritual and temporal power, and there is an overlapping of religious and political policies and law. Thus, theocracies, such as ancient Israel and the Vatican, are states in which religious and political power is indistinguishable. Instead, a state with religious establishment is a political regime in which there is connection both at levels (*i*) and (*iii*), but not at level (*ii*). In such a state, although there is a specific religion (or church) to which formal recognition and privileges are given, representatives of the established religion do not constitute the ruling body.[29]

In a secular *mainstream* (that is, Western) state, no connection exists at the three levels distinguished in the previous paragraph.[30] In fact, in such a state, religion and politics are disconnected in three ways: one, they aim at different ends; two, different persons constitute clergy and public officials; and three, at the level of law and public policies, the state is independent from religious prescriptions. This last level of state–religion

---

[27] Bhargava (2007: 48). The anti-secularists have particularly stressed on the fact that secularism, for its historical origins, is alien to Indian politics and society, among other things. See Madan (1987, 2006, 2010), Nandy (1995), and Nandy and Jahanbegloo (2006).

[28] Bhargava (2009: 89).

[29] Bhargava (2009: 85–8).

[30] Charles Taylor has clearly stressed the cultural particularism of this version of secularism. He maintains that although Westerners tend to extend it universally, such a strong separation between religion and politics has never existed in other moments of human history. In fact, it is a 'product of Latin Christendom and has become part of our way of seeing things in the West'. See Taylor (2011b: 33).

separation is particularly relevant since it gives us the opportunity of distinguishing different versions of secular states. If the separation is seen as one-sided exclusion, we get the 'idealized French conception'[31] of secularism. In French secularism, state and religion are separated, but the former is authorized to interfere in religious matters. According to Bhargava, this conception of secularism entails 'an active disrespect for religion'[32] and has as its sole aim the avoidance of religious dominance over the secular. Bhargava critiques this conception of secularism. For him, although this conception can deal with issues of intra-religious domination, it cannot properly resolve inter-religious domination. This means that though it has resources to oppose those who want to oppress people within a religious group, it is unable to fight the domination of one religious group over others. In practice, French secularism made it possible for no one to be oppressed within religious communities but, at the same time, it could not avoid Catholicism becoming the dominant religion.

However, Bhargava argues, the state–religion separation at the level of law and public policy can also be seen as mutual exclusion. Under this conception, the secular state builds a wall of separation between religion and politics, and neither of the domains is allowed interference in the activities of the other. This version of secularism, labelled 'idealized American model',[33] justifies the state's non-interference in religious affairs with the idea that religion should be a private dimension of an individual's life and that people should be as much free as possible within that sphere. Bhargava rejects this model of secularism too since it can only deal with inter-religious domination. In the American model, the state, through the 'disestablishment of the dominant religion',[34] can only prevent a religious group from dominating other groups. However, the American model is unable to resolve intra-religious domination. In fact, the wall of separation prevents the state from imposing freedom and equality within religious groups. Such separation allows people to leave their existing communities but does not allow them to demand state interference in order to obtain equality within religious groups. In

[31] Bhargava (2011).
[32] Bhargava (2011).
[33] Bhargava (2011).
[34] Bhargava (2011).

practice, the American model prevented that one religious group domi-
nated over the others, but it could not deploy resources to oppose the
violation of individual rights within some religious group.

As might be clear from a reconstruction of Bhargava's arguments, for
him both American and French versions of secularism are inadequate.
Indeed, for Bhargava, an acceptable conception of secularism defends the
separation of religion and politics as an institutional device for making
possible a peaceful social life despite the persistent disagreement in matters of religious truth. Furthermore, secularism has to address in effective
ways the problems of intra and inter-religious domination. The model
that, according to Bhargava, satisfies both these requirements, and is thus
superior to the alternative models just discussed, is the Indian one.

For Bhargava, at the level of law and public policy (level [iii]), the
Indian model of secularism conceives the separation of state and religion
in terms of what he calls *principled distance*. He argues that the Indian
model 'unpacks the metaphor of separation differently'[35] from the traditional Western models. The principled distance model is neither that of a
mutual exclusion (American model) nor as a one-sided exclusion (French
model). The Indian model accepts the fact that the state and religion are
disconnected at the levels of ends and institutions, but 'does not make
a fetish of it at the third level of policy and law'.[36] This means that the
Indian model, at the level of policy and law, does not always recommend a
rigid separation. This is possible, Bhargava contends, due to the centrality
of principled distance within the Indian model of secularism.

The idea of principled distance is premised upon Ronald Dworkin's
notion of treating people as equals, that is, as individuals worthy of equal
concern and respect.[37] In opposition to equal treatment, treating people
as equals might sometimes require differential treatment. Analogous to
Dworkin's view, Bhargava argues that, according to Indian secularism,
principled distance does not demand that the state be equidistant from
all religious groups or that all religious groups be helped or hindered in
exactly the same ways. Principled distance can authorize, in some circumstances, differential treatment of groups. Thus, if required, a state
may interfere sometimes in the affairs of religion. However, a state that

---

[35] Bhargava (2009: 103).
[36] Bhargava (2009: 103).
[37] Dworkin (1978: 125).

intervenes or refrains from interfering with the life of a religious group is not acting upon arbitrary reasons. In fact, the state decides on the requirement of interference or not-intervention 'depending on which of the two better promotes religious liberty and equality of citizenship'.[38] It is very likely that if the state promotes such values in order to fight against both intra and inter-religious domination,[39] policies may affect diverse groups differently. For instance, if the state aims at enhancing social equality, it is bound to intervene much more in the Hindu caste system than in the structures of other religious communities such as Muslims or Christians.

The aforementioned considerations clarify that Bhargava allows for an extensive role for the state. The functions of the state surpass the mere formal guarantee of equal rights. State interventions, Bhargava explicitly claims, are acceptable 'for the sake of substantive values'.[40] Thus, more than a formal notion of equality is at stake here. A similar substantive notion of equality is also fundamental to Chandhoke's conception of Indian secularism.[41] Akin to the conception advocated by Bhargava, Chandhoke demonstrates the distinctive features of the relationship between religion and politics in India. Her theory is complex but, for the purpose of this chapter, can be summarized in the following three statements: (*i*) the state is not attached to any one religion, in the sense that secularism does not acknowledge an official state religion; (*ii*) everyone is free as far as religious beliefs are concerned; and (*iii*) the state ensures 'equality among religious groups by ensuring that one group is not favoured at the expense of another'.[42] However, and this is the most noteworthy aspect of Chandhoke's conception, secularism is a derivative concept. This means that, in order to acquire meaning, secularism has to be grounded in another principle, namely, the principle of substantive equality.[43]

Chandhoke states clearly that 'formal equality is supremely nonchalant about the fact that some religious groups are in a majority, and others

[38] Bhargava (1998b: 515).

[39] Recollect that, for Bhargava, the intra-religious domination and inter-religious domination are among the most serious issues faced by an adequate conception of Indian secularism.

[40] Bhargava (1998b: 520).

[41] Gentile (2015) has remarked the role of equality in Chandhoke's approach.

[42] Chandhoke (1999: 49).

[43] Chandhoke (1999: 88). For a more recent statement, see Chandhoke (2019).

are in a minority.'[44] Mere formal guarantee of equality is not sufficient to fight against existing inequalities. Consider a simple egalitarian distribution of resources among people who are different as far as wealth or well-being is considered. If there were ten baskets of resources to be distributed among ten individuals, a formal egalitarian would give one basket to each individual. It is very likely that, not being sensitive to the prior socio-economic conditions of the recipients, the distribution, rather than reducing the existing inequalities, will reinforce and even exacerbate them. This means that a richer and substantive notion of equality, one that necessitates differential treatment for disadvantaged individuals, is required.

'Proponents of substantive equality', suggests Chandhoke, 'argue for differential treatment of different groups to ensure that disprivileged groups come to acquire some measure of equality with the rest.'[45] Differential treatment is especially required when those individuals or groups are not directly responsible for their disadvantaged condition. Thus, special measures (that is, minority rights) are required to safeguard the interests and avoid the decay of vulnerable minorities and protect their identity from being swamped over by majoritarianism. Note that, for Chandhoke, the state is supposed to apply substantive equality 'both to inter-group as well as intra-group relations'.[46] In this sense, both groups and individuals should be entitled to compensatory measures when they suffer from severe inequalities and disadvantages. Once again, all this makes sure that the state is given extensive powers, and it is just on the basis of these powers that both Bhargava's and Chandhoke's theories will be criticized.

Secularism and the Role of the State in Dealing with Diversity

The pervasive presence of the state in religious affairs is a de facto aspect of Indian society. Such interference is consistent with its constitutional principles. The framers of the Constitution recognized that religious diversity was a defining feature of Indian society and did not try to

---

[44] Chandhoke (1999: 89).
[45] Chandhoke (1999: 91).
[46] Chandhoke (1999: 94).

coercively exclude religion from the public sphere.[47] Beyond mere recognition of religious diversity, the Constitution 'tried to promote equality between different religious communities by acknowledging their separate and distinct character and by protecting the distinctiveness of each'.[48] Note that this is a position perfectly consistent with both Bhargava's and Chandhoke's approaches. Thus, the Constitution, cognizant of the fact of the division of society in majority and minorities, established principles that have allowed the state apparatus to actively interfere in religious matters in order to avoid the dominance of the majority group.

In fact, in the course of the Indian political history, the state made special provisions aimed at protecting the distinctiveness of minority religious groups. Although the political power has abstained from direct intervention in matters of religious worship and belief, it has profoundly regulated the religious practices 'in the interest of protecting public order, morality, and health'.[49] However, given the essential features of South Asian religions (especially Hinduism), permitting state interference in religious practices entails a great concession of power. In fact, unlike Christianity, Hinduism (and Islam to a certain extent) is, as Jeff Spinner-Halev has argued, a 'practice-based' religion. Hinduism, 'lacking a creed and central tenets of faith[,] is concerned with rituals and practices, many of which are social, though some are practiced by individuals'.[50] Thus, granting the state the power to interfere in the practices of Hinduism, even for a noble reason such as the promotion of equality, is a very delicate issue. It means that the state would hold the power to make decisions concerning some crucial aspects of the religion. In this domain, given the relevance of the matters at stake, any abuse or mistake can be particularly severe.

Actually, the Indian state has taken the constitutional provisions to intervene in religious affairs rather seriously. It has been particularly

---

[47] As Rochana Bajpai (2017: 210) has observed, 'in the Constituent Assembly debates, although the term "secularism" was not often used, there were frequent references to a "secular state".... A secular state was not a state that was incognizant of the importance of religious faith in Indian society; nor was it zealous in inculcating skepticism towards religious belief among citizens.'

[48] Mahajan (2008: 300).

[49] Mahajan (2008: 307).

[50] Spinner-Halev (2005a: 35).

proactive in promoting equality, especially among the female and lower-caste populations.[51] For instance, since caste was a reason for excluding people from places of worship, the state has actively prohibited caste-based marginalization. Thus, the state has also legislated 'to regulate and intervene in the functioning of religious institutions',[52] even to decide who can enter into a temple. Thus, the egalitarian thrust of the state has been so strong that, in case of conflict between equality and freedom of religion, the former has often prevailed. This does not mean that religious liberty has been completely revoked, but that in many circumstances it has been subordinated to state constraints and control.

However, what is worrisome and less acceptable, at least from a liberal and individualist perspective such as the one defended in the present book, is the fate of the individual in the case of conflict between equality and freedom of religion. As Mahajan argues, 'on the one hand, religious liberty, particularly the liberty to observe the practices of a community, pushed in the direction of accommodating the concerns of communities ... on the other, the state became the arbiter of the disputes between communities.'[53] This state of affairs has meant that the individual was crushed between two enormous powers, the state and the community. The state, as already remarked, has exercised an enormous power: 'power to negotiate with religious communities, power to take up certain religious and cultural concerns voiced by the members of the community.'[54] The outcome is that the individual loses out since s/he is vulnerable to the power of both the state and the community.

If this brief account of the egalitarian commitment of the state in religious affairs is sound, one might conclude that, at least as far as political practice is concerned, a conception of secularism that is governed by the principle of equality makes possible a strong interventionist state whose policies ended up with objectionable anti-individualist repercussions. Even if one disputes this descriptive account of the functioning of the Indian state concerning religious diversity, conceptions of secularism with a strong egalitarian commitment, such as Bhargava's and Chandhoke's, are still objectionable from a theoretical point of view. In the rest of this

---

[51] Acharya (2008).

[52] Mahajan (2011: 25).

[53] Mahajan (2011: 27).

[54] Mahajan (2011: 27).

section, I will argue that such views of secularism demand much more state intervention than PT liberalism can accept and, for this reason, are severely defective. To prove this, I will consider one at a time the three conditions that make acceptable a state intervention to PT liberalism.[55]

At first glance, Bhargava's and Chandhoke's theories seem to demand a stronger interventionist state than that required by PT liberalism. According to the first condition of legitimate interference in PT liberalism, the state should intervene only when stability and social peace are threatened, and should seek to control the mistreatment of weaker groups by the stronger ones. On their part, Bhargava's and Chandhoke's approaches, relying on strong egalitarian commitments, end up conferring to the state much more power than PT liberalism might accept.

For instance, Bhargava claims that the enforcement of substantive values can authorize the state to intervene in the life of religious groups. Similarly, Chandhoke's notion of substantive equality is very demanding as well. Even leaving aside the difficulties implicit in any attempt to find a common metric of equality in societies marked by deep diversity,[56] when a state assumes equality as the value that should guide its action, it is likely to do more than what is required by the condition of maintenance of peace and order. As a matter of fact, not all inequalities represent a menace to social order. Some inequalities are simply innocuous. In such cases and in many other circumstances, state intervention might exacerbate the situation and generate further problems. Alternatively, it could be useless or, in the worst case, have adverse effects on individuals and groups.[57]

---

[55] These conditions have been listed at the end of the section, 'Beyond the Benign Neglect and Indifference towards Religion'.

[56] See Kukathas (2002b: 194).

[57] Among other considerations, a less interventionist state attitude would be consonant with a crucial feature of Hinduism, namely, the fact that, not being a truth-seeking religion, it looks more for non-interference than having new believers. This signals a crucial difference between Semitic religions and Hinduism. The former conceptualizes itself in terms of universal truths. As S.N. Balagangadhara and Jakob De Roover (2007: 76) write, 'when the (biblical) God reveals His plan, it covers the whole of humankind. Those who receive this revelation should try to convert the others into accepting the message in this divine self-disclosure. That is, proselytizing is an intrinsic drive of Islam and Christianity.' This drive, of course, could create conflicts that a state inspired by the principles of PT liberalism could face, as far as they menace social peace and stability. Instead, to be

The role of the state in exacerbating conflicts (shifting the site of the strife from concrete issues to identity issues) has already been debated in the previous chapter, especially in the section, 'The Archipelago Society and the Politics of Indifference'. Here, I will briefly focus on the possible bad effects of egalitarian policies in religious matters. As a matter of fact, people sometimes join groups whose internal structures are far from egalitarian. In cases like that, pursuing equality may transform those groups into something their members do not accept.[58] The problem is that, as a consequence of the egalitarian transformations, people would feel that they live in an alien environment.

In order to avoid this problem, the proponents of egalitarianism might specify that equality is a principle that should not coercively be imposed on people who might have good reasons for rejecting it. However, even accepting this wariness, the problems for egalitarianism do not cease to exist. As Kukathas has written, there is a more general problem, as 'the point is that equality ... runs aground on the rocks of diversity.'[59] The more a society aims at becoming egalitarian, the more it has to reduce diversity. The fact, basically, is that human diversity hampers equality. Thus, enforcing equality means repudiating diversity.

At this point, one could argue that this repudiation of diversity would not be a serious issue for the perspective defended in this book. In fact, since the first chapter, I have assumed that diversity has no intrinsic value. However, even if diversity has no value in itself, the denial of diversity in favour of equality is still particularly worrisome. As Kukathas argues, '[T]he most important reason for not repudiating diversity is that it is so fundamental a feature of the human condition that any serious attempt to suppress it will lead to injustice and the disruption of individual lives.'[60] Of course, diversity itself is not an unconditional good. Think, for instance, that both at individual and group level, the fact of

---

Hindu is neither a matter of accepting some truths nor a matter of choice: either you are born as Hindu or you are not a Hindu. In this sense, proselytism does not make sense in Hinduism. Thus, as far as Hinduism is concerned, the conflicts engendered by proselytism do not matter.

[58] It is simply in the nature of things that not all the individuals and groups have the same interest in equality.

[59] Kukathas (2002b: 197).

[60] Kukathas (2002b: 191).

diversity produces conflicts. Nonetheless, that individuals and groups tend to differentiate is 'ineradicable'[61] from human conduct and social circumstances. For this reason, conflicts are likewise unavoidable, and it is mainly to manage such conflicts that political institutions are needed.

The conceptions of secularism by Bhargava and Chandhoke also encounter some problems when one considers the second condition of legitimate state intervention according to PT liberalism, the one claiming that the state has to work to render the mainstream society responsive to the needs of all the citizens. The conceptions of Bhargava and Chandhoke are very community centred. They assume that the life of individuals takes place almost exclusively within the community to which they belong. Due to this reason, they do not have an account of the mainstream society in which people from different groups can spend time together. It would seem that Bhargava's and Chandhoke's theories accept both the independence and the completeness assumptions, which have already been proven as defective in the previous chapter.

Thus, the theories I am considering here offer neither a theory on what should be the ideal constitution of the mainstream society, nor an account of what the state should do in order to make it comfortable to the needs of everybody. This entails that Bhargava's and Chandhoke's conceptions of secularism do not have much to say either about the life of individuals beyond their religious groups or about the freedom of exit of an individual from her/his original group. In fact, as argued in the previous chapter, a mainstream society responsive to the needs of a multitude of persons is somehow required by the right of exit. People who dissociate from their group and do not want to adhere to another group should have a place where they can go.

In this regard, someone could argue that, since the freedom to dissociate from a group is not at all crucial for the majority religion in India (Hinduism), the difficulties in accounting for the exit rights are not very worrying for the conceptions of secularism discussed here. As Spinner-Halev has stressed, 'Hinduism is not a voluntary association like Christian churches are, with members and nonmembers. Rather, people are born Hindu; leaving Hinduism is quite difficult,'[62] if not meaningless at all. However, even putting aside the fact that exit rights are not important for

---

[61] Kukathas (2002b: 191).

[62] Spinner-Halev (2005a: 36).

Hinduism, what happens to the rest of the population (approximately 20 per cent), including Muslims and Christians, if someone wants to leave her/his native group and enter into the mainstream society? Additionally, how should one understand the condition of an atheist who does not have a formal religious belonging? The theories of Bhargava and Chandhoke do not provide satisfactory answers to such questions, and hence are quite limited in their scope.

It would seem that Bhargava's and Chandhoke's views fare far better with regard to the third criterion regulating state intervention in PT liberalism. According to this criterion, the state has to guarantee the protection of fundamental individual rights. As remarked earlier, both the theories of Indian secularism discussed in this chapter defend the claim that substantive equality should hold at both inter and intra-group levels. Further, both conceptions agree on the need for the defence of individual rights against the threat of the communities. However, as already demonstrated, in these conceptions, the scope for individualism is severely limited by their pro-community orientation. These conceptions of secularism do not provide adequate channels and the possibility for a right to exit from existing community ties. Individuals are free only within the borders of their groups. Neither the groups nor the state guarantees the inviolability of individual rights when persons decide to dissociate from their groups. Seemingly, this is a severely limited understanding of individual rights.

Thus, notwithstanding the apparent plausibility of Bhargava's and Chandhoke's theories, their conceptualization of state intervention with regard to religious pluralism in India cannot be accepted. Their main weakness does not reside in the idea of state intervention per se, but in their considering religions as the 'handmaidens of justice'.[63] This happens when the political institutions have the power to impose that religious beliefs, practices, and organizations mirror the principles of liberal justice. Thus, since liberal justice advocates autonomy and equality for those who see religions as the 'handmaiden of justice', religious groups should organize their internal life in ways that promote equality and autonomy. However, as already stated in this book, autonomy is not the only way in which human flourishing occurs. An individual can have a good life even living in traditional and non-autonomous groups,

---

[63] Spinner-Halev (2008: 563).

and forcing (in direct or indirect ways) someone to be autonomous can be a form of disrespect for her/his conscience. As Andrew Cohen has written, coercing someone to become autonomous 'would be harming her *as she is* by forcing her to live against her conscience; it would be to discount and set back the interests she currently has without concern for what she wants. ... respecting persons is respecting them *as they are.*'[64] In other words, within PT liberalism, individuals' integrity (namely, the consistency between someone's values and her/his conduct)[65] should be respected, even when it demands illiberal behaviours. Thus, if someone, out of respect for tradition or for countless other reasons, wants to join an illiberal religious group, s/he should be free to do so, and the state should refrain from obstructing her/his choices.

The conclusion is that state interference in religious affairs is not problematic in itself. The actual problem lies rather in the excessive power the conceptions of secularism here presented confer to both the state and religious communities. Political pro-toleration liberalism, as this chapter has shown, provides for an effective theoretical instrument to critique the failings of such theories. This entails that state intervention, even from a minimal liberal perspective such as PT liberalism's, is not to be rejected as such. It should be appropriately constrained.

---

[64] Cohen (2015: 203).
[65] Vallier (2012: 155–60).

7

Conclusion

Synopsis

This book has accomplished two main tasks. First, it has critically reviewed a significant part of the current academic debate on how liberalism deals with diversity. To the possible critical remark that other theories and works could have been discussed, I could reply that the ones presented here have been selected both for scientific relevance and for the fact that they are straightforward examples of the theoretical options I aimed at illustrating. Thus, the reader has been offered a fairly complete overview of the recent philosophical disputes about contemporary liberalism.

Second, after a long analytical process, the book has offered a political theory that ended up as the preferable account of liberalism. Political pro-toleration liberalism, discussed in Chapter 5, represents a viable solution to the complex issues concerning the accommodation of diversity in pluralistic societies. This liberalism, as explained in the text, combines the virtue of a genuine commitment to diversity with the merits of the view that the justification of the liberal assets should be carried out in *political* terms.[1]

The outcome is a theory that emphasizes that liberalism should create the conditions for a peaceful and ordered collective life. This minimal commitment, I contended in the previous chapters, coexists with the view

---

[1] The meaning of political justification has been largely treated in Chapter 1, in the section, 'Liberal Distinctions: Political and Comprehensive, Pro-autonomy and Pro-toleration', and in Chapter 4, in the section, 'The Politicization of Liberalism'.

that, for political purposes, autonomy is not a necessary requisite for the flourishing of human life. This means that, from the point of view of political institutions, people can have a good life even if they accept traditional conceptions of the good and do not behave as perfect autonomous beings, namely, as rational and self-examining individuals. To be more precise, the promotion of autonomy-oriented conceptions of the good life does not fall under the responsibility of a liberal state governed by the precepts of PT liberalism.

In fact, the functions of a liberal state understood along these lines are much more restricted in comparison with other liberal theories. Political pro-toleration liberalism, as argued at the end of Chapter 5, only authorizes state intervention in order to avoid inter-group conflicts, to guarantee that the mainstream society is welcoming to all the individuals and their needs, and to protect basic individual rights. These interventions are aimed at the realization of a peaceful and orderly social life, nothing less and nothing more.

These considerations on the limits of the state intervention are crucial since they avert a situation where PT liberalism ends up with anarchical outcomes:[2] the state, from the theoretical perspective worked out in this book, has some role to play, provided that its actions are not led by the ideal of individual autonomy and are not justified in comprehensive terms, namely, with reference to complex (and controversial) metaphysical, philosophical, and religious issues.[3] Chapters 2, 3, and 4 have proved both the narrowness in terms of accommodation of diversity entailed by the assumption of individual autonomy as the leading value of liberalism and the pitfalls engendered by a comprehensive justification of the liberal order.

Political pro-toleration liberalism, though, is not devoid of any practical import. Chapter 6 has confronted it with the issues raised by religious pluralism in India. This comparison is very challenging given the nature of diversity in the country. In fact, India presents a diversity that is very wide and unknown to the standard Western liberal democratic settings. Thus, a theory that proves to have something to say in such an arduous

---

[2] Remember that Kukathas's theory, from which the discourse on PT liberalism started, admits 'sympathies with (some form) of anarchism'. See Kukathas (2003: 8).

[3] See Note 1.

context has, without a shadow of doubt, many particular merits. Political pro-toleration liberalism, as I argued in Chapter 6, is very helpful when Indian religious pluralism is at stake. In particular, the liberalism I defend in this book has proven to be precious in holding off the intrusiveness of the state power, especially when it is inspired by strong egalitarian commitments. The constraints on the state power are a valuable instrument needed to prevent the bad effects produced by the state itself in the recent history of India.

However, I have to admit that the book has been almost completely silent on a preliminary issue, namely, the *applicability* of liberalism to non-Western contexts such as India. The next section will face this matter and formulate some thoughts on how liberalism, although born in the West, can be acceptable to non-Western people and cultures. Finally, in the last section, I will consider some possible paths of future research that, although neglected in this book, might be opened by the approach worked out here.

The (Alleged) Cultural Particularity of Liberalism

In this section, I will briefly face the following questions: Is the particularistic historical origin of liberalism an obstacle to the acceptance of liberalism itself in contexts different from the West? Are there conditions under which liberalism becomes acceptable also to people who live in non-Western countries?

Bhikhu Parekh is a theorist who has emphasized on the fact that Western liberal democracy is historically determined both as a form of government and as a theory.[4] It is born and has been developed in a specific historical, social, and political context (namely, 'in different parts of Europe from the seventeenth century onwards'[5]). Thus, the *exportation* of liberal democracy to remote settings is not devoid of troubles. The problem, according to Parekh, dwells more in liberalism than in democracy. The latter is a system of government and a set of political institutions aiming at the formulation of collective decisions (namely, free elections, universal suffrage, majority rule, and so on). When understood in these terms, democracy can aspire to be accepted in many and different

---

[4] See also Chakrabarty (2000).
[5] Parekh (1992: 161).

contexts.[6] As a matter of fact, the demand for this kind of democracy is very common in many previously authoritarian countries.[7]

For Parekh, liberalism, instead, is 'historically specific, bound to a particular culture, economy, and polity, and neither travels alone nor lasts long in their absence'.[8] Liberalism, within this account, emphasizes notions such as individualism, personal autonomy, individual rationality, and choice of a moral subject who is completely disembodied and independent from the context in which s/he lives. Further, in this view of liberalism, the relations between state and citizens are not mediated by intermediate institutions such as families, clans, or groups of various sorts.

Liberalism, at least in the way depicted by Parekh, can hardly be accepted by people belonging to those (generally conservative religious) groups that both confer identity to their members and deeply shape their world views. Think, for instance, of what Ayelet Shachar calls 'nomoi groups', namely, those groups that have a constitutive role both in the process of construction of the identity and in the control of the conduct of their members. Nomoi groups can have even texts regulating the public life of the persons belonging to them.[9] For people belonging to such groups, liberal individualism might be not valuable at all. Furthermore, these people do not conceive of their belonging to the political community in individualistic terms. For them, belonging to a group might be more relevant than belonging to a political community. At the most, they could even consider themselves as persons belonging to the political community, but this membership would ultimately be mediated by the prior belonging to the group. This is the case of many groups of migrants who live in liberal democratic settings. Thus, a theory that is unable to accommodate their demands is somehow defective.

However, the liberal model I argue for in this book is quite different from the liberalism Parekh fears and criticizes. The theory I defend is not focused on the protection and promotion of individual autonomy.

---

[6] Note that democracy as a system of government as well as its connections with liberalism have not been discussed in this book.

[7] Consider, for instance, the requests for democracy coming from the countries of the so-called 'Arab Spring'.

[8] Parekh (2011: 81).

[9] See Shachar (2001: 49).

Indeed, as remarked more than once, PT liberalism rejects autonomy as the main liberal commitment. Sure, PT liberalism is individualist, but its individualism only concerns the fact that individuals are the fundamental units of moral and political concerns. The individualism of PT liberalism, I contend, is committed neither to some thick and controversial ontological views about moral personality nor to some sophisticated theories of the action.

Furthermore, PT liberalism acknowledges that individuals can attach great moral and political weight to their groups. As I argued in Chapter 5, individuals owe obligations both to the group to which they belong and to the political society. I have seen these obligations as associative obligations, and nothing was said with the aim of conveying an atomistic conception of the individual.

Thus, it seems that PT liberalism is not vulnerable to the problems faced by liberalism in the version exposed by Parekh. Both the minimalism of commitments and the general parsimony are among the main reasons that render PT liberalism more acceptable and shareable in comparison with the liberalism depicted by Parekh.

However, I think that, in order to dismiss the objection I am considering in this section, it is crucial to stress that liberalism, at least in the version advocated in this book, is a theory of the limits of government action rather than a thick and substantive way of life. Political pro-toleration liberalism, in fact, far from telling people how they should live, sets limits to the power of the state. A state directed by the precepts of PT liberalism does not interfere in the life of individuals to impose controversial conceptions of the good. Such a state has accomplished its tasks once it has ensured that, within a peaceful social environment, basic individual rights are not violated.

Of course, a state ruled according to the principles of PT liberalism does not aim at being universally accepted. It is more easily acceptable for those individuals who, starting from egalitarian and individualistic premises,[10] think that social peace is necessary in order to realize their plans of life. Those who deny these basic assumptions are doubtless beyond the ambit of the persons to which PT liberalism aims at being accepted. In this sense, for instance, Nazis would not accept PT liberalism. On its part, when such groups represent a concrete danger, the state should contain them so that they do not capsize the liberal order.

---

[10] As they have been defined in Chapter 1.

The Inescapable Incompleteness of a Book

All the books are somehow incomplete, in the sense that they do not discuss everything that is worthy to be analysed. There are topics that are simply not addressed because of their irrelevance with regard to the main subject of the book. Then, there is a second set of unaddressed topics, namely, those ones that, although not crucial to the subject of the book, might be developed starting from the work carried out in the book itself.

This book is not an exception to this rather trivial rule. An instance of the first set of unaddressed topics is represented by the institutional arrangement of a liberal state that operates on the basis of the principles of PT liberalism. The reason for the neglect of this issue is that institutional arrangements are beyond the range of interest of a work in political theory such as the present book.

Instead, the distributive implications of PT liberalism are an instance of the second category of issues that have not been discussed. In this book, I mainly deal with how liberalism accommodates diversity and defend a certain account of liberalism. I did not dwell on issues of distributive justice, that is, how the burdens and benefits of social cooperation should be distributed across the members of the society. To be more precise, the book is silent on the possibility of finding an account of social justice[11] that is consistent with PT liberalism and its general stress on diversity.

Here, it is worth to point out that, at present, the effects of diversity on social justice is quite an underdeveloped field of research.[12] Common liberal conceptions of distributive justice, directly or indirectly inspired by the work of John Rawls, have assumed that justice is a virtue of fundamentally homogenous and bounded societies. Actually, the plurality of conceptions of the good and the multiplicity of belongings and loyalties have been somehow acknowledged by contemporary theorists of social justice.[13] However, as David Miller argues, this plurality has mostly been seen as an aspect of the following picture:

> People belong to bounded societies within which the distribution of primary goods—'rights and liberties, opportunities and powers, income and

[11] Here, 'distributive justice' and 'social justice' are used synonymously.
[12] See Miller (2013: 74).
[13] See, for instance, Rawls (1999a), the milestone of the liberal accounts of distributive justice.

wealth'—is governed by a single basic structure, a common set of economic, social and political institutions.[14]

In this representation of society, diversity is recognized, but only up to a certain point. In fact, the ordinary liberal discourse on social justice assumes that individuals, although belonging to different groups, are 'citizens first and foremost'.[15] Thus, their first and prior commitment is to the state, and their 'sense of justice' firstly concerns the state.

The image of society conveyed by PT liberalism, as it has been argued in Chapter 5, is quite different. According to this version of liberalism, people do not make a fetish of the unity of the state. Sure, they owe obligations to the state, but there are obligations to the groups as well. Furthermore, for PT liberalism, contrarily to Rawls's liberalism, justice is not 'the first virtue of social institutions'.[16] More than once I have remarked that, in PT liberalism, institutions are not instruments to enforce autonomy or other controversial conceptions of the good. Here, I would add that the realization of a just society, if justice amounts to compliance to a certain distributive scheme, is not included in the acceptable tasks of the state.

Instead, one could say that for PT liberalism, justice is achieved when individuals are granted an equal opportunity to realize, either individually or within a group, their life plans in a peaceful and ordered social environment. Political pro-toleration liberalism seems not to have direct implications for distributive justice, except that an account of distributive justice should be consistent with the constraints of the state intervention already specified.

These short remarks seem to rule out any consistency between PT liberalism and those theories of distributive justice that develop from Rawls's justice as fairness. However, the consistency between PT liberalism and libertarianism, a view to which PT could easily be accosted, is questionable as well. Libertarianism, with its views of 'thick economic liberty' and of economic rights as moral absolutes,[17] or with its extremely

---

[14] Miller (2013: 71). In this passage, Miller is explicitly referring to Rawls (1999a).

[15] Miller (2013: 73).

[16] Rawls (1999a: 3).

[17] For an understanding of libertarianism as a theory according to which economic rights are moral absolutes, see Brennan and Tomasi (2012) and Tomasi (2012).

strong conception of freedom of contract,[18] is very difficult to reconcile with PT liberalism tenets. In fact, PT liberalism does not say anything about the relevance of economic rights or about the value of freedom of contract. Thus, any libertarian drift of PT liberalism is to be argued for and is, at first glance, quite unlikely also because it goes against the egalitarian general orientation of the theory here defended.

However, as it easy understandable, serious work needs to be done on such issues. My only hope is that this book might serve as a stimulus for this and other future researches.

---

[18] Libertarianism as a theory that stresses the relevance of freedom of contract has been discussed in Freeman (2011). In this article, Freeman (2011: 20) argues that 'libertarians regard freedom of coercively enforceable contracts as of such fundamental importance that it overrides the liberal restriction on the inalienability of basic liberties and also overrides equality of opportunity and equal rights to apply and compete for open positions.'

Bibliography

Abbey, Ruth and Jeff Spinner-Halev. (2013). 'Rawls, Mill, and the Puzzle of Political Liberalism'. *The Journal of Politics* 75(1): 124–36.

Acharya, Ashok. (2008). 'Affirmative Action of Disadvantaged Groups: A Cross-Constitutional Study of India and the US', in R. Bhargava (ed.), *Politics and Ethics of the Indian Constitution*, pp. 267–97. New Delhi: Oxford University Press.

Ackerman, Bruce. (1980). *Social Justice in the Liberal State*. New Haven: Yale University Press.

———. (2004). 'Political Liberalisms', in S.P. Young (ed.), *Political Liberalism: Variations on a Theme*, pp. 79–102. New York: State University of New York Press.

Alam, Javeed. (1998). 'Public Sphere and Democratic Governance in Contemporary India', in R. Bhargava, A.K. Bagchi, and R. Sudarshan (eds), *Multiculturalism, Liberalism and Democracy*, pp. 323–47. New Delhi: Oxford University Press.

Appiah, Kwame A. (2005). *The Ethics of Identity*. Princeton and Oxford: Princeton University Press.

Arneson, Richard J. and Ian Shapiro. (1996). 'Democratic Autonomy and Religious Freedom: A Critique of *Wisconsin* v. *Yoder*', in I. Shapiro, *Democracy's Place*, pp. 137–74. Ithaca, NY: Cornell University Press.

Audard, Catherine. (2009). *Qu'est-ce Que le Libéralisme?: Éthique, Politique, Société*. Paris: Gallimard.

Bader, Veit. (2007). *Secularism or Democracy?: Associational Governance of Religious Diversity*. Amsterdam: Amsterdam University Press.

Bajpai, Rochana. (2011). *Debating Difference: Groups Rights and Liberal Democracy in India*. New Delhi: Oxford University Press.

———. (2017). 'Secularism and Multiculturalism in India: Some Reflections', in A. Triandafyllidou and T. Modood (eds), *The Problem of Religious Diversity: European Challenges, Asian Approaches*, pp. 204–27. Edinburgh: Edinburgh University Press.

Balagangadhara, S.N. and Jakob De Roover. (2007). 'The Secular State and Religious Conflict: Liberal Neutrality and the Indian Case of Pluralism'. *The Journal of Political Philosophy* 15(1): 67–92.

Barry, Brian. (2001). *Culture and Equality: An Egalitarian Critique of Multiculturalism.* Cambridge, MA: Harvard University Press.

Bell, Duncan. (2014). 'What is Liberalism?'. *Political Theory* 42(6): 682–715.

Bellamy, Richard. (2000). 'Dealing with Difference: Four Models of Pluralist Politics'. *Parliamentary Affairs* 53(1): 198–217.

Berlin, Isaiah. (1969). *Four Essays on Liberty.* Oxford: Oxford University Press.

Bhargava, Rajeev. (1998a). 'Introduction', in R. Bhargava (ed.), *Secularism and Its Critics*, pp. 1–28. New Delhi: Oxford University Press.

———. (1998b). 'What Is Secularism For?', in R. Bhargava (ed.), *Secularism and Its Critics*, pp. 486–542. New Delhi: Oxford University Press.

———. (2007). 'The Distinctiveness of Indian Secularism', in T.N. Srinivasan (ed.), *The Future of Secularism*, pp. 20–53. New Delhi: Oxford University Press.

———. (2008). 'Introduction', in R. Bhargava (ed.), *Politics and Ethics of the Indian Constitution*, pp. 1–40. New Delhi: Oxford University Press.

———. (2009). 'Political Secularism: Why It Is Needed and What Can Be Learnt from Its Indian Version', in G.B. Levey and T. Modood (eds), *Secularism, Religion, and Multicultural Citizenship*, pp. 82–109. New York: Cambridge University Press.

——— (2010). *What Is Political Theory and Why Do We Need It?* New Delhi: Oxford University Press.

———. (2011). 'States, Religious Diversity, and the Crisis of Secularism'. *Open Democracy*, available at http://www.opendemocracy.net/rajeev-bhargava/states-religious-diversity-and-crisis-of-secularism-0; 16 September 2019.

Brennan, Jason and John Tomasi. (2012). 'Classical Liberalism', in D. Estlund (ed.), *Oxford Handbook of Political Philosophy*, pp. 115–32. Oxford: Oxford University Press.

Callan, Eamonn. (1997). *Creating Citizens: Political Education and Liberal Democracy.* Oxford: Clarendon Press.

Carens, Joseph. (1987). 'Aliens and Citizens: The Case for Open Borders'. *Review of Politics* 49(2): 251–73.

———. (2005). 'The Integration of Immigrants'. *Journal of Moral Philosophy* 2(1): 29–46.

———. (2013). *The Ethics of Immigration.* Oxford: Oxford University Press.

Carr, Craig L. (2010). *Liberalism and Pluralism: The Politics of E pluribus Unum.* New York: Palgrave Macmillan.

Ceva, Emanuela. (2005). 'Liberal Pluralism and Pluralist Liberalism'. *Res Publica* 11(2): 201–11.

Chakrabarty, Dipesh. (2000). *Provincializing Europe: Postcolonial Thought and Historical Difference.* Princeton: Princeton University Press.

Chandhoke, Neera. (1999). *Beyond Secularism.* New Delhi: Oxford University Press.

———. (2019), *Rethinking Pluralism, Secularism and Tolerance: Anxieties of Coexistence.* New Delhi: Sage.

Citrin, Jack and John Sides. (2008). 'Immigration and the Imagined Community in Europe and the United States'. *Political Studies* 56(1): 33–56.

Cohen, Andrew Jason. (2015). 'Contemporary Liberalism and Toleration', in S. Wall (ed.), *The Cambridge Companion to Liberalism*, pp. 189–211. Cambridge: Cambridge University Press.

Crowder, George. (2002). *Liberalism and Value Pluralism*. New York: Continuum.

———. (2004). *Isaiah Berlin: Liberty and Pluralism*. Cambridge: Polity Press.

———. (2007). 'Two Concepts of Liberal Pluralism'. *Political Theory* 35(2): 121–46.

———. (2013). *Theories of Multiculturalism: An Introduction*. Cambridge: Polity Press.

Crowder, George and Henry Hardy (eds). (2007). *The One and the Many: Reading Isaiah Berlin*. Amherst, NY: Prometheus Books.

Deveaux, Monique. (2000). *Cultural Pluralism and the Dilemmas of Justice*. Ithaca: Cornell University Press.

Dewey, John. (1923). 'The School as a Means of Developing Social Consciousness and Social Ideas in Children'. *Journal of Social Forces* 1(5): 513–17.

———. (1934). *A Common Faith*. New Haven: Yale University Press.

Donatelli, Piergiorgio. (2006a). 'Bringing Truth Home: Mill, Wittgenstein, Cavell and Moral Perfectionism', in A. Norris (ed.), *The Claim to Community: Essays on Stanley Cavell and Political Philosophy*, pp. 38–57. Stanford: Stanford University Press.

———. (2006b). 'Mill's Perfectionism'. *Prolegomena* 5(2): 149–64.

Dostert, Troy. (2006). *Beyond Political Liberalism: Toward a Post-Secular Ethics of Public Life*. Notre Dame: University of Notre Dame Press.

Dworkin, Ronald. (1978). 'Liberalism', in S. Hampshire (ed.), *Public and Private Morality*, pp. 113–43. Cambridge, MA: Cambridge University Press.

———. (1986). *Law's Empire*. Fontana: London.

———. (2000). *Sovereign Virtue: The Theory and Practice of Equality*. Cambridge, MA: Harvard University Press.

———. (2011). *Justice for Hedgehogs*. Cambridge, MA: Belknap Press.

Ferrara, Alessandro. (2014). *The Democratic Horizon: Hyperpluralism and the Renewal of Political Liberalism*. New York: Columbia University Press.

Festenstein, Matthew. (2000). 'Cultural Diversity and the Limits of Liberalism', in N. Sullivan (ed.), *Political Theory in Transition*, pp. 70–90. New York: Routledge.

———. (2005). *Negotiating Diversity: Culture, Deliberation, Trust*. Cambridge: Polity Press.

Fish, Stanley. (1999). 'Mutual Respect as a Device of Exclusion', in Stephen Macedo (ed.), *Deliberative Politics: Essays on Democracy and Disagreement*, pp. 88–102. New York; Oxford: Oxford University Press.

Fitzmaurice, Deborah. (1993). 'Autonomy as a Good: Liberalism, Autonomy, and Toleration'. *The Journal of Political Philosophy* 1(1): 1–16.

Frazer, Michael L. (2007). 'John Rawls: Between Two Enlightenments'. *Political Theory* 35(6): 756–80.

Freeman, Samuel. (2007). *Rawls*. New York: Routledge.

———. (2011). 'Capitalism in the Classical and High Liberal Traditions'. *Social Philosophy and Policy* 28(2): 19–55.

Galeotti, Anna E. (2002). *Toleration as Recognition*. Cambridge, MA: Cambridge University Press.

Galston, William A. (1982). 'Defending Liberalism'. *The American Political Science Review* 76(3): 621–9.

———. (1988). 'Liberal Virtues'. *The American Political Science Review* 82(4): 1201–16.

———. (1989). 'Civic Education in the Liberal State', in N. Rosenblum (ed.), *Liberalism and Moral Life*, pp. 89–101. Cambridge, MA: Harvard University Press.

———. (1991). *Liberal Purposes*. New York: Cambridge University Press.

———. (1995). 'Two Concepts of Liberalism'. *Ethics* 105(3): 516–34.

———. (2002a). *Liberal Pluralism: The Implications of Value Pluralism for Political Theory and Practice*. Cambridge: Cambridge University Press.

———. (2002b). 'Review of S. Macedo, *Diversity and Distrust: Civic Education in a Multicultural Democracy*'. *Ethics* 112(2): 386–91.

———. (2004). 'Liberal Pluralism: A Reply to Talisse'. *Contemporary Political Theory* 3(1): 140–7.

———. (2005). *The Practice of Liberal Pluralism*. Cambridge, MA: Cambridge University Press.

———. (2006). 'À Propos de *The Practice of Liberal Pluralism* de William Galston: Un Dialogue avec l'Auteur'. *Les Ateliers de l'Éthique* 1(1): 112–27.

———. (2007a). 'Must Value Pluralism and Religious Belief Collide?', in G. Crowder and H. Hardy (eds), *The One and the Many: Reading Isaiah Berlin*, pp. 251–62. Amherst, NY: Prometheus Books.

———. (2007b). 'Why the New Liberalism Isn't All that New, and Why the Old Liberalism Isn't What We Thought It Was'. *Social Philosophy and Policy* 24(1): 289–305.

———. (2009). 'What Value Pluralism Means for Legal–Constitutional Orders'. *San Diego Law Review* 46(4): 803–18.

———. (2010). 'Realism in Political Theory'. *European Journal of Political Theory* 9(4): 385–411.

———. (2011). 'Parents, Government, and Children: Authority over Education in a Pluralist Liberal Democracy'. *Law and Ethics of Human Rights* 5(2): 284–305.

———. (2013). 'Between Logic and Psychology: The Links between Value Pluralism and Liberal Theory'. *The Review of Politics* 75(1): 97–101.

Gentile, Valentina. (2015). 'Secularism in Plural Post-colonial Democracies: Is Liberal Toleration Enough?', in P. Losonczi and W. Van Herck (eds), *Politics, Religion, Secularisation: India and Europe*, pp. 65–84. New Delhi: Routledge.

Gilbert, Margaret. (2006). *A Theory of Political Obligations*. Oxford: Oxford University Press.

Gill, Emily R. (2001). *Becoming Free: Autonomy and Diversity in the Liberal Polity*. Lawrence, KS: University Press of Kansas.

Gray, John. (1996). *Isaiah Berlin*. Princeton: Princeton University Press.

———. (2000a). 'Where Pluralists and Liberals Part Company', in M. Baghramian and A. Ingram (eds), *Pluralism: The Philosophy and Politics of Diversity*, pp. 85–102. London: Routledge.

———. (2000b). *Two Faces of Liberalism*. New York: New Press.

Green, Leslie. (1995). 'Internal Minorities and their Rights', in W. Kymlicka (ed.), *The Rights of Minority Cultures*, pp. 256–72. New York: Oxford University Press.

Greene, Abner S. (2012). *Against Obligation: The Multiple Sources of Authority in a Liberal Democracy*. Cambridge, MA: Harvard University Press.

Gutmann, Amy. (1980). 'Children, Paternalism, and Education: A Liberal Argument'. *Philosophy and Public Affairs* 9(4): 338–58.

———. (1999). *Democratic Education*, Second Edition. Princeton: Princeton University Press.

———. (2004). 'Unity and Diversity in Democratic Multicultural Education: Creative and Destructive Tensions', in J.A. Banks (ed.), *Diversity and Citizenship Education: Global Perspectives*, pp. 71–98. San Francisco: Jossey-Bass.

Haidar, Hamid H. (2008). *Liberalism and Islam: Practical Reconciliation between the Liberal State and Shiite Muslims*. New York: Palgrave Macmillan.

Hampshire, Stuart. (1983). *Morality and Conflict*. Cambridge, MA: Harvard University Press.

Hart, Herbert L.A. (1955). 'Are There Any Natural Rights?'. *Philosophical Review* 64(2): 175–91.

———. (1961). *The Concept of Law*. Oxford: Clarendon.

Hasan, Zoya. (2005). 'The Shah Bano Affair', in *Encyclopedia of Women & Islamic Cultures*, Vol. 2, pp. 740–4. Leiden: Brill.

Hirst, Paul Q. (ed.). (1989). *The Pluralist Theory of the State: Selected Writings of G.D.H. Cole, J.N. Figgis and H.J. Laski*. London: Routledge.

Horton, John. (2010). *Political Obligation*, Second Edition. Basingstoke: Palgrave Macmillan.

Jayal, Niraja Gopal. (2006). *Representing India: Ethnic Diversity and the Governance of Public Institutions*. New York: Palgrave Macmillan.

Joppke, Christian. (2010). *Citizenship and Immigration*. Cambridge: Polity Press.

Kant, Immanuel. (1970). *The Critique of Pure Reason*. New York: St. Martin's Press.

Kaviraj, Sudipta. (2014). 'Modernity, State, and Toleration in Indian History', in C. Taylor and A. Stepan (eds), *Boundaries of Toleration*, pp. 233–66. New York: Columbia University Press.

Kekes, John. (1996). *The Morality of Pluralism*. Princeton: Princeton University Press.
Kishwar, Madhu. (1999). 'Politics as Majoritarianism vs. Minoritarianism', in D.L. Sheth and G. Mahajan (eds), *Minority Identity and Nation State*, pp. 138–68. New Delhi: Oxford University Press.
Klosko, George. (1987). 'Fairness and Political Obligations'. *Ethics* 97(2): 353–62.
———. (2004). *The Principle of Fairness and Political Obligation*, Second Edition. Lanham: Rowman & Littlefield.
Kukathas, Chandran. (1995). 'Are There Any Cultural Rights?', in W. Kymlicka (ed.), *The Rights of Minority Cultures*, pp. 228–56. Oxford: Oxford University Press.
———. (1996). 'Liberalism, Communitarianism, and Political Community'. *Social Philosophy and Policy* 13(1): 80–105.
———. (1997a). 'Multiculturalism as Fairness: Will Kymlicka's *Multicultural Citizenship*'. *The Journal of Political Philosophy* 5(4): 406–27.
———. (1997b). 'Liberalism, Multiculturalism, Oppression', in A. Vincent (ed.), *Political Theory: Tradition and Diversity*, pp. 132–53. Cambridge: Cambridge University Press.
———. (1998). 'Liberalism and Multiculturalism: The Politics of Indifference'. *Political Theory* 26(5): 686–99.
———. (1999). 'Tolerating the Intolerable'. *Papers on Parliament* 33: 67–81.
———. (2000). 'Two Concepts of Liberalism', in J.C. Espada, M.A. Plattner, and A. Wolfson (eds), *The Liberal Tradition in Focus: Problems and New Perspectives*, pp. 97–110. Oxford: Lexington Books.
———. (2002a). 'The Life of Brian, or Now for Something Completely Difference-Blind', in P. Kelly (ed.), *Multiculturalism Reconsidered: 'Culture and Equality' and Its Critics*, pp. 184–203. Cambridge: Polity Press.
———. (2002b). 'Equality and Diversity'. *Politics, Philosophy, and Economics* 1(2): 185–212.
———. (2003). *The Liberal Archipelago: A Theory of Diversity and Freedom*. Oxford: Oxford University Press.
———. (2005). 'The Case for Open Borders', in A.I. Cohen and C.H. Wellman (eds), *Contemporary Debates in Applied Ethics*, pp. 207–20. London: Blackwell.
———. (2006). 'Rights of Culture, Rights of Conscience', in R. Tinnevelt and G. Verschraegen (eds), *Between Cosmopolitanism and State Sovereignty*, pp. 109–19. Basingstoke: Palgrave Macmillan.
Kymlicka, Will. (1989a). *Liberalism, Community, and Culture*. Oxford: Clarendon Press.
———. (1989b). 'Liberal Individualism and Liberal Neutrality'. *Ethics* 99(4): 883–905.
———. (1995). *Multicultural Citizenship: A Liberal Theory of Minority Rights*. Oxford: Oxford University Press.

————. (1996a). 'Social Unity in a Liberal State'. *Social Philosophy and Policy* 13(1): 105–36.

————. (1996b). 'Two Models of Pluralism and Tolerance', in D. Heyd (ed.), *Toleration: An Elusive Virtue*, p. 81–105. Princeton: Princeton University Press.

————. (1998). *Finding Our Way: Rethinking Ethnocultural Relations in Canada.* Oxford: Oxford University Press.

————. (2001a). *Politics in the Vernacular: Nationalism, Multiculturalism, Citizenship.* Oxford: Oxford University Press.

————. (2001b). 'Territorial Boundaries: A Liberal Egalitarian Perspective', in D. Miller and S.H. Hashmi (eds), *Boundaries and Justice: Diverse Ethical Perspectives*, pp. 249–75. Princeton: Princeton University Press.

————. (2002). *Contemporary Political Philosophy: An Introduction.* Oxford: Oxford University Press.

————. (2004). 'Dworkin on Freedom and Culture', in J. Burley (ed.), *Dworkin and His Critics*, pp. 113–33. Malden, MA: Blackwell.

————. (2007a). 'The Global Diffusion of Multiculturalism: Trends, Causes, Consequences', in S. Tierney (ed.), *Accommodating Cultural Diversity*, pp. 17–34. Aldershot: Ashgate.

————. (2007b). 'The New Debate on Minority Rights (and Postscript)', in A.S. Laden and D. Owen (eds), *Multiculturalism and Political Theory*, pp. 25–59. Cambridge UK: Cambridge University Press.

————. (2007c). *Multicultural Odysseys: Navigating the New International Politics of Diversity.* Oxford: Oxford University Press.

————. (2009). 'The Governance of Religious Diversity: The Old and the New', in P. Bramadat and M. Koenig (eds), *International Migration and the Governance of Religious Diversity*, pp. 1–12. Montreal and Kingston: McGill-Queen's University Press.

————. (2012). *Multiculturalism: Success, Failure, and the Future.* Washington, DC: Migration Policy Institute.

Larmore, Charles E. (1987). *Patterns of Moral Complexity.* Cambridge, UK: Cambridge University Press.

————. (1990). 'Political Liberalism'. *Political Theory* 18(3): 339–60.

————. (1996). *The Morals of Modernity.* Cambridge, UK: Cambridge University Press.

Leavis, F.R. (ed.). (1962). *Mill on Bentham and Coleridge.* London: Chatto & Windus.

Levy, Jacob T. (2003). 'Liberalism's Divide, After Socialism and Before'. *Social Philosophy and Policy* 20(1): 278–97.

Macedo, Stephen. (1990). *Liberal Virtues: Citizenship, Virtue, and Community in Liberal Constitutionalism.* Oxford: Clarendon Press.

————. (1995a). 'Liberal Civic Education and Religious Fundamentalism: The Case of God v. John Rawls'. *Ethics* 105(3): 468–96.

————. (1995b). 'Liberal Civic Education and Its Limits'. *Canadian Journal of Education* 20(3): 304–14.

————. (1996). 'Community, Diversity, and Civic Education: Toward a Liberal Science of Group Life'. *Social Philosophy and Policy* 13(1): 240–68.

————. (1998). 'Transformative Constitutionalism and the Case of Religion: Defending the Moderate Hegemony of Liberalism'. *Political Theory* 26(1): 56–80.

————. (2000a). *Diversity and Distrust: Civic Education in a Multicultural Democracy.* Cambridge, MA: Harvard University Press.

————. (2000b). 'In Defense of Liberal Public Reason: Are Slavery and Abortion Hard Cases?', in R.P. George and C. Wolfe (eds), *Natural Law and Public Reason*, pp. 11–49. Washington, DC: Georgetown University Press.

————. (2007). 'The Moral Dilemma of US Immigration Policy: Open Borders vs. Social Justice?', in C. Swain (ed.), *Debating Immigration*, pp. 63–81. Cambridge, MA: Cambridge University Press.

————. (2010). 'Ragione Pubblica, Democrazia e Comunità Politica: Un Riesame Delle Critiche'. *Filosofia e questioni pubbliche* 14(1): 23–50.

MacIntyre, Alasdair. (1984). *After Virtue: A Study in Moral Theory.* Notre Dame: University of Notre Dame Press.

MacKinnon, Catharine A. (2006). 'Sex Equality under the Constitution of India: Problems, Prospects, and "Personal Laws"'. *International Journal of Constitutional Law* 4(2): 181–202

Maclure, Jocelyn and Charles Taylor. (2011). *Secularism and Freedom of Conscience.* Cambridge, MA, and London: Harvard University Press.

MacMullen, Ian. (2007). *Faith in Schools?: Autonomy, Citizenship, and Religious Education in the Liberal State.* Princeton: Princeton University Press.

Madan, Triloki N. (1987). 'Secularism in Its Place'. *The Journal of Asian Studies* 46(4): 747–59.

————. (2006). *Images of the World: Essays on Religion, Secularism, and Culture.* New Delhi: Oxford University Press.

————. (2010). 'Indian Secularism: A Religio-secular Ideal', in L.E. Cady and E.S. Hurd (eds), *Comparative Secularism in a Global Age*, pp. 181–96. New York: Palgrave Macmillan.

Maffettone, Sebastiano. (2010). *Rawls: An Introduction.* Cambridge: Polity Press.

Mahajan, Gurpreet. (2005a). 'Can Intra-group Equality Co-exist with Cultural Diversity?: Re-examining Multicultural Frameworks of Accommodation', in A. Eisenberg and J. Spinner-Halev (eds), *Minorities within Minorities: Equality, Rights and Diversity*, pp. 90–112. Cambridge: Cambridge University Press.

————. (2005b). 'Indian Exceptionalism or Indian Model: Negotiating Cultural Diversity and Minority Rights in a Democratic Nation-State', in W. Kymlicka and B. He (eds), *Multiculturalism in Asia*, pp. 288–313. Oxford: Oxford University Press.

————. (2008). 'Religion and the Indian Constitution: Questions of Separation and Equality', in R. Bhargava (ed.), *Politics and Ethics of the Indian Constitution*, pp. 297–310. New Delhi: Oxford University Press.

————. (ed.). (2011). *Accommodating Diversity: Ideas and Institutional Practices*. New Delhi: Oxford University Press.

————. (2014). 'Religious Diversity and Multicultural Accommodation', in S. Sikka and L.G. Beaman (eds), *Multiculturalism and Religious Identity: Canada and India*, pp. 55–75. Montreal and Kingston: McGill-Queen's University Press.

March, Andrew. (2006). 'Liberal Citizenship and the Search for an Overlapping Consensus: The Case of Muslim Minorities'. *Philosophy and Public Affairs* 34(4): 373–421.

————. (2007). 'Islamic Foundations for a Social Contract in Non-Muslim Liberal Democracies'. *American Political Science Review* 101(2): 235–52.

Marshall, T.H. (1965). *Class, Citizenship, and Social Development*. Garden City, NY: Anchor.

Melidoro, Domenico. (2014). 'The Principles of Secularism: Is the Clash among Principles Necessary?' *Ragion Pratica* 38(1): 233–46.

Mill, John Stuart. (2003). *Utilitarianism and On Liberty*. Malden, MA: Blackwell.

Miller, David. (2005). 'Immigration: The Case for Limits', in A.I. Cohen and C. H. Wellman (eds), *Contemporary Debates in Applied Ethics*, pp. 193–206. London: Blackwell.

————. (2008). 'Immigrants, Nations, and Citizenship'. *The Journal of Political Philosophy* 16(4): 371–90.

————. (2013). *Justice for Earthlings: Essays in Political Philosophy*. Cambridge, UK: Cambridge University Press.

————. (2016). *Strangers in Our Midst: The Political Philosophy of Immigration*. Cambridge, MA: Harvard University Press.

Mitra, Subatra K. (2013). 'Multicultural Nationhood and the State in India', in J. Tripathy and S. Padmanabhan (eds), *The Democratic Predicament: Cultural Diversity in Europe and India*, pp. 59–94. New Delhi: Routledge.

Modood, Tariq. (2013). *Multiculturalism*, Second Edition. Cambridge: Polity Press.

Mohapatra, Bishnu N. (2010). 'Minorities and Politics', in N.G. Jayal and P.B. Metha (eds), *The Oxford Companion to Politics in India*, pp. 219–37. New Delhi: Oxford University Press.

Moon, J. Donald. (1993). *Constructing Community: Moral Pluralism and Tragic Conflicts*. Princeton: Princeton University Press.

Moore, Margaret. (2001). *The Ethics of Nationalism*. Oxford: Oxford University Press.

Mullally, Siobhan. (2004). 'Feminism and Multicultural Dilemmas in India: Revisiting the *Shah Bano* Case'. *Oxford Journal of Legal Studies* 24(4): 671–92.

Murphy, Michael. (2012). *Multiculturalism: A Critical Introduction*. New York: Routledge.

Nandy, Ashis. (1995). 'An Anti-secular Manifesto'. *India International Centre Quarterly* 22(1): 35–64.

Nandy, Ashis and Ramin Jahanbegloo. (2006). *Talking India: Ashis Nandy in Conversation with Ramin Jahanbegloo*. New Delhi: Oxford University Press.

Newman, Dwight G. (2003). 'Liberal Multiculturalism and Will Kymlicka's Uneasy Relation with Religious Pluralism'. *Bijdragen: International Journal in Philosophy and Theology* 64(3): 265–85.

Nozick, Robert. (1974). *Anarchy, State, and Utopia*. New York: Basic Books.

Nussbaum, Martha. (1999). 'A Plea for Difficulty', in S.M. Okin, *Is Multiculturalism Bad for Women?*, pp. 105–14. Princeton: Princeton University Press.

———. (2001). 'India: Implementing Sex Equality through Law'. *Chicago Journal of International Law* 2(1): 35–58.

———. (2011). 'Perfectionist Liberalism and Political Liberalism'. *Philosophy and Public Affairs* 39(1): 3–45.

Okin, Susan Moller. (1999). *Is Multiculturalism Bad for Women?* Princeton: Princeton University Press.

O'Neill, Onora. (1989). *Constructions of Reason: Explorations in Kant's Practical Philosophy*. New York: Cambridge University Press.

Parekh, Bhikhu. (1992). 'The Cultural Particularity of Liberal Democracy'. *Political Studies* 40(Special Issue): 160–75.

———. (2006). *Rethinking Multiculturalism: Cultural Diversity and Political Theory*. New York: Palgrave Macmillan.

———. (2008). *A New Politics of Identity: Principles for an Interdependent World*. New York: Palgrave Macmillan.

———. (2011). *Talking Politics*. New Delhi: Oxford University Press.

Pasolini, Pier Paolo. (1996). *Poems*, selected and translated by Norman MacAfee with Luciano Martinengo. New York: Farrar, Straus and Giroux.

Patten, Alan. (2012). 'Liberal Neutrality: A Reinterpretation and Defence'. *Journal of Political Philosophy* 20(3): 249–72.

Pevnick, Ryan. (2011). *Immigration and the Constraints of Justice: Between Open Borders and Absolute Sovereignty*. Cambridge, MA: Cambridge University Press.

Phillips, Anne. (2007). *Multiculturalism without Culture*. Princeton: Princeton University Press.

Quong, Johnathan. (2014). 'On the Idea of Public Reason', in J. Mandle and D. Reidy (eds), *A Companion to Rawls*, pp. 265–80. Oxford: Wiley-Blackwell.

Rawls, John. (1997). 'The Idea of Public Reason Revisited'. *University of Chicago Law Review* 64(3): 765–807.

———. (1999a). *A Theory of Justice*, Revised Edition. Cambridge, MA: Harvard University Press.

———. (1999b). *Collected Papers*. Cambridge, MA: Harvard University Press.

———. (2005). *Political Liberalism*, Expanded Edition. New York: Columbia University Press.

Raz, Joseph. (1990). 'Facing Diversity: The Case of Epistemic Abstinence'. *Philosophy & Public Affairs* 19(1): 3–46.

———. (1994). *Ethics in the Public Domain*. Oxford: Oxford University Press.

Ryan, Alan. (2012). *The Making of Modern Liberalism*. Princeton: Princeton University Press.

Şahin, Bican. (2010). *Toleration: The Liberal Virtue*. Lanham: Lexington Books.

Sandel, Michael. (1982). *Liberalism and the Limits of Justice*. Cambridge: Cambridge University Press.

Seth, Sanjay. (2001). 'Liberalism, Diversity and Multiculturalism'. *The Indian Journal of Political Science* 62(3): 321–33.

Shachar, Ayelet. (2001). *Multicultural Jurisdictions: Cultural Differences and Women's Rights*. Cambridge: Cambridge University Press.

———. (1998). 'Group Identity and Women's Rights in Family Law: The Perils of Multicultural Accommodation'. *The Journal of Political Philosophy* 6(3): 285–305.

Shklar, Judith. (1989). 'The Liberalism of Fear', in N. Rosenblum (ed.), *Liberalism and Moral Life*, pp. 21–38. Cambridge, MA: Harvard University Press.

Simmons, John A. (1979). 'The Principle of Fair Play'. *Philosophy and Public Affairs* 8(4): 307–37.

———. (2001). *Justification and Legitimacy: Essays on Rights and Obligations*. Cambridge: Cambridge University Press.

Spinner-Halev, Jeff. (1994). *The Boundaries of Citizenship: Race, Ethnicity, and Nationality in the Liberal State*. Baltimore: Johns Hopkins University Press.

———. (1995). 'Difference and Diversity in an Egalitarian Democracy'. *The Journal of Political Philosophy* 3(3): 259–79.

———. (1999). 'Cultural Pluralism and Partial Citizenship', in C. Joppke and S. Lukes (eds), *Multicultural Questions*, pp. 65–86. Oxford: Oxford University Press.

———. (2000). *Surviving Diversity: Religion and Democratic Citizenship*. Baltimore: Johns Hopkins University Press.

———. (2001). 'Feminism, Multiculturalism, Oppression and the State'. *Ethics* 112(1): 84–113.

———. (2005a). 'Hinduism, Christianity, and Liberal Religious Toleration'. *Political Theory* 33(1): 28–57.

———. (2005b). 'Autonomy, Association, Pluralism', in A. Eisenberg and J. Spinner-Halev (eds), *Minorities within Minorities: Equality, Rights, and Diversity*, pp. 157–71. Cambridge: Cambridge University Press.

———. (2008). 'Liberalism and Religion: Against Congruence'. *Theoretical Inquiries in Law* 9(2): 553–72.

Talisse, Robert B. (2004). 'Can Value Pluralists be Comprehensive Liberals?': Galston's Liberal Pluralism'. *Contemporary Political Theory* 3(1): 127–39.

———. (2011). *Pluralism and Liberal Politics*. New York, NY, and Abingdon, UK: Routledge.

Tate, John William. (2013). '"We Cannot Give One Millimeter"? Liberalism, Enlightenment, and Diversity'. *Political Studies* 61(4): 1–18.

Taylor, Charles. (1985). 'Atomism', in C. Taylor, *Philosophy and the Human Sciences: Philosophical Papers, Vol. 2*, pp. 187–210. Cambridge: Cambridge University Press.

———. (1992). 'The Politics of Recognition', in A. Gutmann (ed.), *Multiculturalism: Examining the Politics of Recognition*, pp. 25–73. Princeton: Princeton University Press.

———. (2011a). 'Why We Need a Radical Redefinition of Secularism', in E. Mendieta and J. Vanantwerprn (eds), *The Power of Religion in the Public Sphere*, pp. 34–59. New York: Columbia University Press.

———. (2011b). 'Western Secularity', in C. Calhoun, M. Juergensmeyer, and J. Van Antwerpen (eds), *Rethinking Secularism*, pp. 31–53. Oxford: Oxford University Press.

———. (2014). 'How to Define Secularism', in C. Taylor and A. Stepan (eds), *Boundaries of Toleration*, pp. 59–78. New York: Columbia University Press.

Ten, Chin L. (1993). 'Multiculturalism and the Value of Diversity', in C. Kukathas (ed.), *Multicultural Citizens: The Philosophy and Politics of Identity*, pp. 7–16. Sydney: Centre for Independent Studies.

Tomasi, John. (2001). *Liberalism beyond Justice: Citizens, Society, and the Boundaries of Political Theory*. Princeton: Princeton University Press.

———. (2012). *Free Market Fairness*. Princeton: Princeton University Press.

Tripathy, Jyotirmaya and Sudarsan Padmanabhan. (2013). 'Introduction', in J. Tripathy and S. Padmanabhan (eds), *The Democratic Predicament: Cultural Diversity in Europe and India*, pp. 1–35. New Delhi: Routledge.

Vallier, Kevin. (2012). 'Liberalism, Religion and Integrity'. *Australasian Journal of Philosophy* 90(1): 149–65.

Van der Vossen, Bas. (2011). 'Associative Political Obligation'. *Philosophy Compass* 6(7): 477–87.

Waldron, Jeremy. (1987). 'Theoretical Foundations of Liberalism'. *Philosophical Quarterly* 37(147): 127–50.

———. (2004). 'Liberalism, Political and Comprehensive', in G.F. Gaus and C. Kukathas (eds), *Handbook of Political Theory*, pp. 89–99. London: Sage.

Walzer, Michael. (1983). *Spheres of Justice*. New York: Basic Books.

Weinstock, D.M. (1997). 'The Graying of Berlin'. *Critical Review* 11(4): 481–501.

———. (2007). 'Liberalism, Multiculturalism, and the Problem of Internal Minorities', in A.S. Laden and D. Owen (eds), *Multiculturalism and Political Theory*, pp. 244–64. Cambridge: Cambridge University Press.

————. (2008). 'Value Pluralism, Autonomy, and Toleration', in H.S. Richardson and M.S. Williams (eds), *Moral Universalism and Pluralism: Nomos XLIX*, pp. 125–48. New York: New York University Press.

Williams, Bernard. (1978). 'Introduction', in H. Hardy (ed.), *Concepts and Categories: Philosophical Essays by Isaiah Berlin*, pp. xiii–xx. London: Hogarth Press.

Wolfe, Cristopher. (2006). *Natural Law Liberalism*. Cambridge, UK: Cambridge University Press.

Young, Shaun P. (2002). *Beyond Rawls: An Analysis of the Concept of Political Liberalism*. Lanham, MD: University Press of America.

Zakaras, Alex. (2013). 'A Liberal Pluralism: Isaiah Berlin and John Stuart Mill'. *The Review of Politics* 75(1): 69–96.

Index

About the Author

Domenico Melidoro is a lecturer at the Department of Political Science, and a researcher at the Ethos Research Center, Luiss University of Rome, Italy. An expert in liberalism, secularism, and practical ethics, he has published numerous essays in national and international journals. He is the author of *Multiculturalismo. Una piccola introduzione* [*Multiculturalism: A Short Introduction*] (2015).